DAMN NEAR PERFECT™
COCKTAILS

DOUG BERDIE, PhD

Wisdom
Editions

MINNEAPOLIS

Minneapolis

First Edition March 2025

Damn Near Perfect™ Cocktails. Copyright © 2025 by Doug Berdie.
All rights reserved.

10 9 8 7 6 5 4 3 2 1
ISBN: 978-1-962834-39-1

Cover and book design by Gary Lindberg
Photography by Phil Eckhert

Contents

INTRODUCTION

The original intent of this project was to "perfect" a dozen or so cocktails that my wife Elaine and I could enjoy when the mood struck us for a certain type of drink. When friends heard about our project, they insisted we send them copies of the recipes.

We decided to add amateur photos taken with my mobile phone. After seeing them, our good friend Phil Eckhert offered to retake the photos to spruce things up. All the while, other people, including total strangers who overheard us talking, insisted they wanted copies of the recipes. That interest from others led us to publish a book of thirty recipes with the design help of Elise Walker.

The continued interest over the past ten years has led us to refine several of the initial thirty recipes and to add twenty-five new favorites.

We are not professional bartenders. We are a couple who enjoy well-made cocktails and learning to make them ourselves. We were pleased to learn that others do too.

Earnie Larsen, who, for many years, was a respected counselor in the area of recovery from addictive behaviors, used to say, "Perfection is not an option." Keeping that in mind lightens one's life. My wife Elaine and I no longer strive to be perfect—we strive, instead, to be "Damn Near Perfect" or, as we often say, "DNP."

The prayer contained in Appendix Seven helps define why Damn Near Perfect is better than perfection. Hence, this edition presents fifty-five cocktails we believe are Damn Near Perfect (DNP). They are the best we have achieved to date.

It's likely the cocktails can be improved further. If you believe you have done so, we would love to hear the changes you have made. Please send them to me at dberdie@calumeteditions.com.

The following cocktail recipes were created using the scientific method—testing, retesting, testing yet again—all with variations to the recipes and using blind tastings to eliminate biases associated with brand names and ingredient amounts. This method is what differentiates our recipes from many found in other cocktail books and online. A more complete description of the method we follow is in Appendix Two.

Important: When judging cocktails (especially ones like Sazerac that are almost all whiskey) the first sip doesn't count! The first sip of a spirit, as opposed to tasting wine, floods the taste buds with alcohol. After your first sip, wait a few seconds before taking the second sip. Listen to your taste buds and you will be surprised at how many more flavors you can discern in the second sip.

We encourage you to start testing cocktails. Invite friends to taste and evaluate a variety of cocktails, and as Maya Angelou said in her cookbook, Great Food, all day long, "It must be remembered that a good friend does not allow a guest to drive after too much alcohol. So have a good time and be wise."

Cheers!

ANCHO MAGNÍFICO

The Ancho Magnífico is a Mexican-style cocktail that highlights the taste of the chile poblano and does so in a way that is not excessively spicy. Tajín® rimming salt is more widely available than it used to be in Mexican grocery stores and upscale liquor stores, as well as online.

- 1 oz. Ancho Reyes Verde™ Chile Poblano Liqueur
- 1½ oz. mescal[1]
- 1 oz. blackberry syrup
- ¾ to 1 oz. lime juice
- 1 mint sprig (3 or 4 leaves) plus a couple additional ones
- ¼-inch slice of moist lime
- Tajín® clásico rim salt

1. In a cocktail shaker, pour the Ancho Reyes Verde™ liqueur, mescal, blackberry syrup, lime juice, and 1 mint sprig. Muddle lightly and stir well for 30 seconds.

2. Moisten rim of cocktail glass with a piece of lime and dip in a plate of Tajín® rimming salt to lightly coat the glass rim.

3. Add 5 or 6 ice cubes to the cocktail shaker and shake vigorously for 30 to 40 seconds.

4. Put 3 or 4 new ice cubes in the rimmed glass and strain the shaken mixture into it.

5. Add additional mint leaves as ornament.

The above measures yield **one** Ancho Magnífico DNP™ cocktail.

NOTES

[1] Sacrificio® reposado is an excellent mescal for this cocktail because it's not overly smoky.

ANTHONY QUINN

Many recipes exist for this cocktail. We were introduced to it on a Seabourn™ cruise and enjoyed it so much we fiddled and fiddled to make a version we really like. The biggest challenge is finding a good passion fruit puree or making it yourself.

- 1 basil leaf
- 1½ oz. white rum[1]
- ¾ oz. passion fruit puree[2]
- ⅜ oz. cinnamon syrup
- ½ oz. lime juice
- 1 egg white — we recommend pasteurized
- 1½ oz. sparkling water

1. Either make a passion fruit puree by pureeing pieces of fresh or thawed passion fruit or buy premade.

2. Make (or buy) the cinnamon syrup by crushing 5 cinnamon sticks and adding them to a pan with 8½ oz. of superfine (i.e., baker's) sugar and 8½ oz. of hot water (just below a boil). Simmer for 5 minutes and strain carefully. Cool.

3. Muddle the basil leaf in a cocktail shaker, then add all the remaining ingredients except the sparkling water.

4. Shake to get the egg white foamy. Add 3 or 4 ice cubes and shake again. Strain into previously chilled glass, being sure to scoop out some egg foam into the glass. Pour in 1½ oz. of sparkling water and stir lightly. Adorn with a basil leaf.

The above measures yield **one** DNP™ Anthony Quinn cocktail.

NOTES

[1] Many white rums are just fine. We like Rhum J.M for this cocktail.

[2] Jungle Pulp™ passion fruit pulp (available on the internet) works very well here.

APPLE CIDER–HOT SPICED

This is a wonderful cocktail for a chilly winter evening. It really warms the innards of three cold folks. The key is to be sure the mugs have been warmed sufficiently to keep the cocktail hot.

- 4 cups fresh apple cider[1]
- 4 black peppercorns
- 4 cinnamon sticks (divided 3 and 1)
- 3 whole cloves
- 1 star anise
- 3 ¼-inch orange slices (cut in half)
- 3 ¼-inch slices of a crisp apple (cut in half), 1 slice of each per drink
- 4½ oz. good bourbon (1½ oz. per cocktail)[2]

1. Fill three mugs with very hot water. Let them sit so they warm the mugs well.
2. Put the apple cider, peppercorns, one cinnamon stick, the cloves, and the star anise in a medium saucepan. Bring to a boil. Lower the heat and simmer for 5 minutes.
3. Then empty the mugs and let sit 60 seconds. Strain the mixture from the pan into the mugs (one-third into each mug).
4. Drop an orange slice and an apple slice into each mug, add 1½ oz. of bourbon into each mug. Stir each mug with a cinnamon stick, then drop it into the mug. Hang another of the orange slices over the edge of the cup if you wish.

The above measures yield **three** DNP™ Apple Cider–Hot Spiced cocktails.

NOTES

[1] If you can't find fresh cider (i.e., in the refrigerated section of the supermarket), Martinelli's Gold Medal Cider™ off the shelf works very well.

[2] Wolcott Single Barrel Bourbon® works well.

APPLETINI

Many versions of Appletinis are now served. The use of Minnesota-grown Honeycrisp apples is what elevates ours to DNP status. Juice the apples through an electric juicer, carefully skim off the foam with a spoon, then strain the juice several times through dampened cheesecloth. You will achieve a clear liquid that is more elegant than what other apples, or bottled juices, yield.

- 2½ oz. vodka[1]
- 2 oz. Bak's Bison Grass Vodka®
- ¾ oz. apple liqueur[2]
- ¾ oz. Noilly Prat® original dry vermouth
- 3 oz. freshly juiced apple juice (from Honeycrisp apples if possible)[3]
- Nutmeg, cut in half, ready to grate
- ¼-inch slice of apple (cut on a mandoline or with a very sharp knife) with a slit cut in it, or a very thin whole round slice

1. Pour first five ingredients into a shaker with lots of ice.
2. Shake 40 to 50 times.
3. Strain into two chilled, large Martini glasses.
4. Using a Microplane®, grate the nutmeg across it 3 or 4 times so a bit of the grating is on the top of the drink.
5. Hang the ¼-inch slice of apple on the rim of the glass or float a whole slice over the drink and serve.

The above measures yield **two** DNP™ Appletini cocktails served in large Martini glasses.

NOTES

[1] We prefer Smirnoff® No. 21 red-label vodka.

[2] We prefer Schönauer® Apfel. Berentzen®. is a second choice. Do not substitute Calvados for the apple liqueur. It does not work well.

[3] If you do not have an electric juicer you may be forced to use juice from a grocery store. Juicing six apples by machine, and carefully filtering with cheesecloth, yields about 11 ounces of juice. If you freeze the juice into ice cube trays that have giant 3-oz. ice cube holes, each cube, when thawed, will yield two cocktails. It's a great way to treasure this cocktail over many months.

BLOODY MARY

The Bloody Mary is a legendary cocktail that is delightful any time of year, at any time of day, and almost all guests love this cocktail. It requires a good rimming salt, though, so be sure to sip it from the glass rim and forgo the urge to use a straw.

- Good salt for rimming the glass, made especially for Bloody Marys[1]
- 8 oz. Zing Zang™ Bloody Mary mix[2]
- 2 oz. vodka[3]
- Squirt of lime juice
- Celery stalk
- Lemon peel
- Dill pickle on a stick (optional)

1. Rub rim of a 12-oz. glass with lime slice and dip into salt mixture that has been spread onto plate.
2. Put 2 or 3 ice cubes in the glass. Add the Zing Zang™, vodka, and lime juice.
3. Stir well with celery stalk, add optional dill pickle (if desired), and serve.

ALTERNATIVE

- 2 oz. vodka[3]
- 2 oz. tomato juice
- ¼ oz. lemon juice
- 1 tsp. Worcestershire sauce
- 2 dashes celery bitters
- Pinch of sea salt
- Pinch of cayenne
- Pinch of black pepper

1. Fill a 12-oz. glass with ice.
2. Put all the alternative ingredients in a cocktail shaker filled with ice. Shake 30 times and strain into ice-filled glass. Garnish with celery stalk, lemon peel, and dill pickle (if desired).

Each of the above techniques yield **one** DNP® Bloody Mary cocktail.

NOTES

[1] We have a strong preference for J.Q. Dickenson salt.

[2] Zing Zang™ is the very best premixed version we've tried.

[3] We prefer Smirnoff® No. 21 red-label vodka.

BOOTLEGGER

This cocktail is legendary among Twin Cities' country clubs—and makes a refreshing drink after eighteen holes of golf on a hot, humid day. The recipe is, supposedly, a closely guarded secret. Nonetheless, we believe our recipe stands up well to any of the country club versions. We prefer vodka, though some people prefer gin or rum.

- 1 cup relatively small mint leaves, packed tightly, but not jammed in
- 12 oz. frozen lemonade concentrate—just the concentrate, no water)[1]
- 1½ oz. vodka or gin[2]
- 5 oz. club soda
- Mint sprig for garnish

1. Put the first two ingredients in a blender and blend well. Pulse to get the best blend.

2. Refrigerate for 3 to 4 days for the best result so the mint can steep, shaking occasionally.

3. Strain through a fine strainer or a coarse strainer set over a double layer of dampened cheesecloth. Makes syrup for many drinks and can be used at once or refrigerated for a week.

4. In a tall 12-oz. glass with 5 or 6 ice cubes, pour 2 oz. of the strained mint syrup, vodka, and 5 oz. of club soda. Stir well.

5. Add mint sprig for garnish and serve with a straw.

The above measures yield **one** DNP™ Bootlegger cocktail served in a large highball glass.

NOTES

[1] We use Minute Maid® frozen concentrate.

[2] We prefer Smirnoff® No. 21 red-label vodka. We prefer Gordon's™ gin (*not* lime-infused).

BOULEVARDIER

This cocktail is becoming more and more popular. It's tasty and very easy to make. However, if you are a person who does not like tartness in your cocktail, you may not enjoy this one.

- 1½ oz. bourbon or rye[1]
- ¾ oz. Campari™ (or Aperol™ for less "bite")
- ¾ oz. sweet vermouth
- Orange twist for garnish

1. Stir the first three ingredients in a rocks glass with two ice cubes.
2. Strain over ice into a different rocks glass. Stir a bit more.
3. Garnish with orange twist.

The above measures yield **one** DNP™ Boulevardier cocktail.

NOTES
[1] Michter's Single Barrel Straight Rye™ works beautifully.

BRANDY ALEXANDER WITH CREAM

This is a wonderful after-dinner cocktail. Great variation exists in what is served at bars and restaurants. It is much easier to find than its ice cream relative. Some say it was named after Czar Alexander II; others say it was named after New York City Prohibition bartender Troy Alexander. Who knows?

- 1 oz. brandy[1]
- 1 oz. dark crème de cacao[2]
- 2 oz. heavy cream—not ultra-pasteurized
- Fresh nutmeg, cut in half, for rubbing across a Microplane®, for garnish
- Hazelnut, for garnish

1. Pour the first three ingredients into a cocktail shaker filled with eight ice cubes and shake about 40 times.
2. Strain into a small Martini glass.
3. Garnish with the grated nutmeg sprinkled over the top, and place hazelnut in the center.

The above measures yield **one** DNP™ Brandy Alexander with Cream cocktail served in small Martini glass.

NOTES

[1] We prefer Remy Martin® VSOP Cognac for our brandy; Hennessey® V.S. also works well.

[2] We use De Kuyper® for the dark crème de cacao.

BRANDY ALEXANDER WITH ICE CREAM

This wonderful, decadent cocktail once was easy to find in upscale steak and chop restaurants but no longer is. As one seasoned bartender told us with a grin, "When someone asks for a Brandy Alexander with ice cream, we say, 'The blender is broken.'" Other bartenders have been heard to say, "If we can't shake it, we won't make it." Our fond memories of this cocktail led us to experiment until we arrived at the following DNP version.

- 1½ oz. dark crème de cacao[1]
- 1 oz. brandy[2]
- ½-pint vanilla ice cream[3]
- ½ cup crushed ice
- Fresh nutmeg (cut in half) for rubbing across a Microplane™
- Hazelnut for garnish

1. Put the first four ingredients in a blender. Cover and frappé until consistency of a good milkshake.
2. Pour into brandy snifters or other glass of preference.
3. Garnish with the grated nutmeg sprinkled over the top, and place hazelnut in the center.

The above measures yield **two** DNP™ cocktails.

NOTES

[1] We use De Kuyper® for the dark crème de cacao.

[2] We prefer Remy Martin® VSOP Cognac for our brandy; Hennessey® V.S. also works well.

[3] We really prefer Graeter's® or Haagen-Dazs® to other ice creams. Some others leave a bitter aftertaste. Lactaid™, a lactose-free dairy product, works well, too.

BROOKLYN BONFIRE

The Brooklyn Bonfire is fun to prepare in front of your guests. Be sure you do not lean over the fire when you flame the cocktail (so you don't burn your eyebrows as I once did when flaming another dish).

- 2 oz. nice bourbon[1]
- 1½ chartreuse[2]
- ⅓ tsp sweet vermouth
- 10 drops (or one dash) cherry bark vanilla bitters
- Cocktail cherry for garnish

1. Pour all ingredients (except the cherry) into a mixing glass with ice and mix well.
2. Invert a cocktail coupe glass (the type shown in the photo).
3. Either light the end of a hickory stick, then blow it out and quickly slip it under the inverted glass so it fills with smoke, leaving the glass upside down touching the table so the smoke stays in it, or use the Smoking Gun® by Breville, or similar, to create the smoke and follow the same action.
4. Flip the glass over and while the smoke is escaping, pour the previously mixed cocktail into the glass.

The above measures yield **one** DNP™ cocktail.

NOTES

[1] Evan Williams™ single barrel works very well.

[2] We prefer green Chartreuse™.

CABLE CAR

We've enhanced this Sidecar relative to fit our tastes. It's a San Francisco classic invented by Tony Abou-Ganim in the Starlight Room at the Drake Hotel. Our enhancements include using dry Curaçao (instead of standard Curaçao) and using Meyer lemons, which have a more elegant flavor than standard lemons.

- Glass rimming mixture:
   ¼ tsp. ground cinnamon
   ¾ Tbs. superfine sugar
- 1 cup ice cubes
- 5 Tbs. spiced rum[1]
- 2 Tbs. 2:1 simple syrup (2 cups water to 1 cup sugar)
- ⅛ cup Meyer lemon juice (it's too hard to regulate regular lemon juice)
- 3 Tbs. dry orange Curaçao[2]
- 1 orange peel ¼-inch to ½-inch wide, 1-inch long; all pith removed)
- 1 ice cube per glass (optional)

1. Rub the rim of glasses with Meyer (or regular) lemon juice and dip into plate of well-mixed rimming mixture to get a light coating. Set glasses in freezer to chill.
2. Fill cocktail shaker halfway with ice and add spiced rum, simple syrup, Meyer lemon juice, and dry orange Curaçao. Shake vigorously 40 times. Strain into rim-coated chilled glasses. Drop in ice cube (if desired), squeeze orange peel over drink, and drop it in. (Adding an ice cube will loosen the cocktail a bit.)

The above measures yield **two** DNP™ Cable Car cocktails served in small Martini or Sherry glasses.

NOTES

[1] We like Sailor Jerry's® or Captain Morgan® rum.

2 We prefer Pierre Ferrand® Dry Curaçao because plain orange Curaçaos make a slightly "thicker," overly sweet version.

2 We prefer Pierre Ferrand® Dry Curaçao because plain orange Curaçaos make a sligl "thicker," overly sweet version.

CAIPIRINHA

The Caipirinha is a, or perhaps *the*, great cocktail of Brazil. It varies a lot depending on the cachaça that is used (and what is available where you live), so it's worth trying whatever you can find to get it just the way you like it. And, if you get to Brazil, be sure to try a wide variety of them.

- ½ oz. fresh lime juice
- Peel from ½ lime w/all white pith removed
- ½ oz. 1:1 simple syrup
- 3 oz. cachaça[1]
- Lime wheel slice for garnish

1. Fill rocks glass with 4 or 5 ice cubes to chill (or put in freezer for a while).
2. In a cocktail shaker, muddle the lime peel with the lime juice and the simple syrup.
3. Add cachaça and one cup of ice cubes and shake vigorously 40 times.
4. Strain into rocks glasses with fresh ice cubes and garnish with lime wheel slice.

The above measures yield **one** DNP™ Caipirinha cocktail.

NOTES

[1] Our personal preferences are Ypioca™ 161, Corote, and Ypioca™ Ouro. Unfortunately, we've only been able to find the last two in the US. Ypioca™ 161 is the most nuanced.

CHAMPAGNE COCKTAIL

This is a very basic Champagne Cocktail. Many bartenders put a drop or so of Angostura® bitters on the sugar cube; we, however, prefer this DNP™ version without the bitters. It's best with real French Champagne (we use Piper Heidsieck® NV) but it also works reasonably well with higher-quality California (or other) sparkling wines.

- 1 white sugar cube per glass
- 1 Tbs. cognac[1]
- 7 oz. Champagne

1. Put a sugar cube in the bottom of a Champagne tulip or flute glass the appropriate size to hold the ingredients. (Some flutes only hold 4½ oz. so be sure you have something that will hold about 8 oz.).
2. Add cognac.
3. Fill glass with Champagne—pouring slowly down the side of the glass so it doesn't foam over.

The above measures yield **one** DNP™ Champagne cocktail served in a Champagne flute.

NOTES

[1] We like Remy Martin® VS. VS.

CHURCHILL REVISITED

The Churchill Revisited cocktail has many variations and is based on Winston Churchill's legendary love of Scotch whiskey. We tried many versions using bourbon and using Scotch as the whiskey, and our preferred recipes are shown below. It would be wise for you to try your own versions, as the results we obtained are slightly different from each other, and you'll want to find what best suits your palate.

- 2 oz. bourbon[1] or 1½ oz. Scotch[2]
- ½ oz. lime juice
- ½ oz. Cointreau
- ½ oz. sweet vermouth
- ¼ tsp 1:1 simple syrup
- Twist of lime

1. Blend all ingredients except the lime twist in a cocktail shaker and shake with 3 or 4 ice cubes 20 to 30 times.
2. Serve with the twist of lime.

The above measures yield **one** DNP™ Churchill Revisited cocktail.

NOTES

[1] We find Woodward Reserve™—Double Oaked, and Wolcott™ both work well. Others may too.

[2] Dewars™ is a fine blended Scotch for this cocktail. VS.

COSMOPOLITAN FAMILY

The Cosmopolitan is a classic cocktail based on vodka, Cointreau®, lime juice, and cranberry juice. In addition to the classic Cosmo, we've included two variations of which we are very fond: the Cherrypolitan and the Shanghai Cosmo. All three versions of the Cosmopolitan are on the following pages. Try each of the three.

CHERRYPOLITAN

The Cherrypolitan, one of our DNP variations on the Cosmopolitan, is a real hit with our friends. The Cherrypolitan does not replace the Cosmopolitan on our drink list, both are available depending on the moods of our guests. People who prefer a cocktail that is slightly more tart than the Cosmo really like this alternative. The cocktail is enhanced if you use fresh pitted cherries that have been washed, dried, and frozen for 6 to 8 months. They add a nice, almost liqueur-like character. Thaw and remove the pits using a pitting tool so the cherries are not annihilated. If you haven't planned ahead, try Bada Bing Cherries® available in some upscale grocery stores and most liquor stores rather than maraschino cherries.

- 1½ oz. Citroen Vodka[1]
- ½ oz. Cointreau®
- ¼ oz. fresh lime juice
- 1 oz. tart cherry juice[2] (or you can use pomegranate juice, such as POM® or Lakewood® for a nice variation)
- Martini glass (chilled in freezer)
- Two pitted cocktail cherries

1. Put a few ice chips in each glass.
2. Put first four ingredients in a cocktail shaker filled with ice cubes and shake vigorously 40 to 50 times. Let sit for 20 seconds or so. Pour through strainer into the prepared Martini glass.
3. Put two pitted cherries on a split plastic pick and hang them on the rim of the glass so the pick is half inside and half outside the glass rim, or lay the cherries on a pick across the glass rim.

The above measures yield **one** DNP™ cocktail served in a small Martini glass.[3]

NOTES

[1] We like Ketel One Citroen® Vodka.

[2] We prefer R.W. Knudsen® organic "Just Tart Cherry." Some other cherry juices are too sweet for this cocktail.

[3] Tripling the recipe nicely fills two large Martini glasses.

COSMOPOLITAN

This is our Damn Near Perfect® version of the many recipes for the classic Cosmopolitan. Much debate exists over the history of this cocktail and who created it.

- 1½ oz. Citroen vodka[1]
- ½ oz. Cointreau®
- ¼ oz. fresh lime juice
- 1 oz. cranberry juice[2]
- Two small Martini glasses (chilled in refrigerator or freezer)
- Orange peel (¼-inch to ½-inch wide; 1-inch long; all pith removed; twisted)

1. Put a few ice chips in each glass.
2. Put first four ingredients in a cocktail shaker filled with ice and shake vigorously 40 to 50 times. Let sit for 20 seconds or so. Pour through a strainer into the prepared Martini glasses.
3. Twist an orange peel over the drink and hang on the side of the rim.

The above measures yield **two** DNP™ cocktails served in small Martini glasses.[3]

NOTES

[1] We like Ketel One Citroen® vodka.

[2] We prefer Ocean Spray® Cranberry Juice Cocktail to other more austere cranberry juices.

[3] Tripling the recipe nicely fills two large Martini glasses.

COSMOPOLITAN–SHANGHAI

The Shanghai Cosmo is delightful any time of the year and almost all guests love this cocktail. We are always sure to have cranberry juice in the house so we can make this cocktail whenever the desire hits us.

- 1½ oz. vodka[1]
- 1 oz. plum wine/sake[2]
- 1 Tbs. fresh lime juice
- 1 oz. cranberry juice[3]
- 1 Tbs. guanabana juice (i.e., soursop juice)[4]
- 1 Tbs. pineapple juice (fresh is best)
- Cherry and lemon twist for garnish with optional piece of pineapple.

1. Chill a large Martini glass in freezer for 10 to15 minutes.
2. Put all liquids in cocktail shaker with 5 or 6 ice cubes and shake 40 times.
3. Put a few ice chips in the chilled Martini glass and pour the mixture over it. Squeeze lemon twist over mix and drop in or hang over edge along with optional piece of pineapple. Add cherry.

The above measures yield **one** DNP™ Shanghai Cosmo cocktail.

NOTES

[1] We like Smirnoff #21™.

[2] Our preference is Plum Fu-Kui™.

[3] We prefer Ocean Spray® Cranberry Juice Cocktail to other more austere cranberry juices.

[4] Foco™, Goya™, Jump, and Phillipine brands all work well. In a pinch, canned coconut juice works well too.

EAST INDIA COCKTAIL

The East India Cocktail is an innovative, refreshing cocktail with ingredients that are not often joined. Making the pineapple syrup is easy and adds to the taste of the cocktail. It keeps well in the refrigerator.

- Pineapple syrup:
  ½ cup sugar
  1 cup water
  1 cup pureed pineapple chunks
- 2 oz. Cognac[1]
- ¼ oz. maraschino liqueur[2]
- 1 tsp Dry Curaçao[3]
- ⅛ tsp. Angostura bitters
- 1 tsp. pineapple syrup (see above)
- 1 lemon twist for garnish

1. Make the pineapple syrup by combining sugar and water and bringing to a boil. Stir until sugar is dissolved and syrup thickens. Add pureed pineapple chunks. Stir and simmer for 10 minutes. Cool and strain through fine mesh.

2. Mix 1 tsp. of pineapple syrup with all other ingredients (except lemon twist) in a cocktail shaker with 6 or 7 ice cubes. Shake 50 times.

3. Strain into chilled cocktail glass with at least two regular sized ice cubes.

4. Garnish with lemon twist.

The above measures yield **one** DNP™ East India Cocktail.

NOTES

[1] We use Courvoisier VSOP.

[2] We use Luxardo™, or juice from a Luxardo™ Cherries jar.

[3] We prefer Pierre Ferrand.

EL PRESIDENTE

The El Presidente is, perhaps, our favorite response to the question either of us might ask: "What should we have tonight for our evening cocktail?" We've been told it's a favorite cocktail to present to Cuban dignitaries. If so, it's obvious why.

- 1½ oz. aged rum[1]
- ¼ oz. dry vermouth[2]
- ¼ oz. Cointreau™ (no other orange-flavored sweetener is as good for this)
- ½ tsp. grenadine[3]
- Orange peel, 1 to 2 inches long, all pith removed, for garnish

1. Fill a mixing glass with ice to let it chill.
2. Add rum, vermouth, Cointreau™, and grenadine. Stir vigorously for 40 seconds.
3. Strain into a cocktail glass containing one ice cube if you wish; rub rim with orange peel and drop it in.

The above measures yield **one** DNP™ cocktail.

NOTES

[1] Our very favorite rum, after many taste tests, is Metusalem™ Gran Reserve. Flor de Cana Nicaraguan 12-year-old (and even the 7-year-old) is an excellent alternative. And Angostura Rum is a nice alternative, although it presents a very different, yet excellent, taste.

[2] We like Dolin vermouth for this cocktail.

[3] It's important to use the homemade version of grenadine in Appendix One. Commercial grenadine is too sweet.

GIN AND TONIC

Gin and Tonic cocktails evoke memories of hot days, languorous afternoons sitting on porches chatting, and other ways of pleasantly passing the time. Certain times cry out for this cocktail. As we continue to enjoy our DNP™ Gin and Tonic cocktail, we will also continue to test and tinker with it, given the spate of new gins and new tonics becoming available.

- 1½ to 2 oz. Beefeater® gin
- Schweppes® tonic (*not* diet)
- Small wedge of lime (or lemon if you prefer)

1. Place six ice cubes in an 11- or 12-ounce highball glass.
2. Squeeze lime (or lemon) wedge into glass and drop in.
3. Add gin (amount according to your preference).
4. Fill glass with tonic and stir lightly.

The above measures yield **one** DNP™ cocktail.

Finding the DNP™ GIN AND TONIC

Testing this cocktail is difficult because of all the ingredients: gin brand, tonic brand, lime vs. lemon, water ice cubes vs. tonic cubes, and the amounts. In dozens of tastings, we learned the following:

1. Some tonics have strong tastes of their own (e.g., Fentimans® and Fever-Tree®); others are neutral (e.g., the tonic Q®); and yet others are in the middle (e.g., Schweppes®, Canada Dry®).

2. Some tonics are better by themselves, and others are better with gin. For example, Fentimans® tastes good all by itself but fights with gin, leading to an unbalanced result. Schweppes® is too sweet by itself, but we like it when gin and lime or lemon are added.

3. We had more trouble than with any other cocktail agreeing on which tested version we prefer. This indicates that your own preference may not be that of others. For example: Elaine's #1 gin with Schweppes® or Canada Dry® tonics is Beefeater®, while mine is Tanqueray®.

4. Some gins go better with certain tonics, and with other tonics it does not matter which gin is used. For example, with Fever Tree® tonic our favorite gin pairings are Bombay Sapphire®, Bombay®, and Tanqueray® gins—which we like equally. With Q® tonic, we both clearly prefer Beefeater® gin.

5. Although it was not our #1 choice for some tonics, we like Beefeater® gin with all tonics, and it would be a fine choice for any tonic that may be available.

6. If one makes ice cubes from leftover tonic (to use instead of water ice cubes), the tonic used will affect the outcome. A sweeter tonic (such as Schweppes®) will make the cocktail grow sweeter as the cubes dissolve, whereas a tonic like Q® will have less of that effect.

7. Finally, most people in the US prefer a lime wedge, while many in other parts of the world prefer lemon. This is something each of you should experiment with to find your own preference.

The bottom line is, simple as they may appear, finding a DNP™ Gin and Tonic is highly personal and will take individual testing.

HOT CHOCOLATE WITH DECADENT BUTTERED RUM

This is a delicious cocktail to enjoy on a cold evening (or a warm one for that matter). The recipe below will yield enough for four to six smaller mugs or two very large ones.

- ½ cup (1 stick) softened butter
- 2 oz. bittersweet chocolate, chopped
- ½ cup packed light brown sugar
- 1 tsp. ground cinnamon
- ⅛ tsp. kosher salt
- ¾ cup dark rum[1]
- ½ cup heavy cream
- Freshly ground nutmeg

1. Pour boiling water in the serving mugs so they get nice and hot.
2. Melt the butter and chocolate in a medium bowl in microwave (with bursts of 15-second heat and stirs), or in a double boiler, stirring until smooth.
3. Whisk the brown sugar, cinnamon, and salt into the butter-chocolate mixture.
4. Bring 2½ cups of water to a boil in a medium saucepan.
5. Remove from heat and whisk in the rum and the chocolate mixture.
6. Beat cream until soft peaks. Reheat chocolate (if needed). Empty the cups of hot water, divide the drinks into the cups, and top with whipped cream. Sprinkle grated nutmeg over top.

The above measures yield **two** to **four** DNP™ Hot Chocolate Rum drinks.

NOTES

[1] Myers's™ is excellent for this cocktail.

JULIET AND ROMEO

This fun DNP™ cocktail is a crowd pleaser. It differs depending on the gin. We prefer an English gin for this one as opposed to American gins that, generally, have less juniper.

- 3 sprigs of fresh spearmint (not peppermint), plus one small leaf for garnish)
- 3 slices fresh cucumber, peeled[1]
- Very tiny pinch of sea salt (3 or 4 grains)
- 2 oz. English gin[2]
- ¾ oz. 2:1 simple syrup (2 cups water to 1 cup sugar)
- ½ oz. fresh lime juice
- 3 drops rose water (plus one additional drop at end)
- 3 drops Angostura® bitters (plus three additional drops at end)
- Marie Antoinette Champagne glass

1. In a small glass or cocktail shaker, gently muddle the mint, cucumber, and salt.
2. Add gin, simple syrup, lime juice, 3 drops of rose water, and 3 drops of Angostura® bitters. Stir, and let stand 30 seconds.
3. If muddled and mixed in a glass, pour into a cocktail shaker.
4. Add 7 or 8 ice cubes, shake 40 times, and strain into glass (small bits of mint are okay, but make sure the cucumber seeds do not get through the strainer).
5. Drop three drops Angostura® bitters on top of the cocktail.
6. Place one drop of rose water in the center of the glass, then place a small mint leaf on top of the rose water drop.

The above measures yield **one** DNP™ Juliet and Romeo cocktail.

NOTES

[1] Do not use hothouse or English cucumbers as they tend not to be juicy enough.

[2] We prefer Bombay Sapphire® gin for this cocktail. Bols Genever® makes a very different but tasty version.

LIMONCELLO

Most Limoncello we've had at Italian restaurants and bars has been too sweet for our taste. Elaine developed this version (based on a variety of sources), which is less sweet, and the nuances are apparent. It makes a wonderful after-dinner or before-bed cocktail. It does take a lot of work, but it can be refrigerated (and enjoyed) for many weeks, even months, so it's worth the effort.

- 2 lbs. lemons
- 1 Qt. vodka[1]
- 5 cups of purified water
- 1½ cups cane sugar (preferred), or granulated

1. Use a fine grater to zest the lemons. Put the zest and vodka in a jar large enough to hold 1-plus quarts of liquid. Tightly seal. Store in a cool, dark place 3 to 5 days.

2. Shake jar at least twice per day. Zest will be white when flavoring is optimum.

3. Strain zest out with a very fine sieve and discard. Set aside the lemon vodka you've made.

4. Heat 5 cups of water over low heat in a saucepan. Add sugar and heat, stirring until syrup is clear. Cool to room temperature and mix with lemon vodka.

5. Strain sweetened lemon vodka through coffee filters 6 times (it takes a long time!). Refrigerate in tightly sealed bottle(s). Enjoy chilled!

These measures yield enough DNP™ Limoncello cocktails to serve many.

NOTES

[1] We like Smirnoff #2™.

MAI TAI

A good Mai Tai is very hard to find. Most are overly sweet and syrupy. Our version is a tropical paradise in a glass. The key is the falernum used and a bit of Absente®. Thanks go to Mike Rizzo for the general recipe, and to Paul Clarke for inspiring our slightly altered falernum.

- ¼ cup water
- 1½ Tbs. lime juice
- 1 Tbs. 2:1 simple syrup (2 cups water to 1 cup sugar)
- 2 Tbs. fresh grapefruit juice (pink is best). One grapefruit yields about 7 oz.
- 2 Tbs. dark rum[1]
- 3 Tbs. golden rum[2]
- 1 Tbs. Cointreau®
- 1 Tbs. Falernum syrup[3]
- ½ tsp. Angostura® bitters
- ¼ tsp. Absente® (or Pernod®)
- Pineapple slice
- Cocktail cherry

1. Shake first ten ingredients with ice and strain into a glass filled with ice cubes.
2. Garnish with pineapple slice and cocktail cherry. We prefer Bada Bing Cherries® over maraschinos.
3. Serve with a straw.

The above measures yield **one** DNP™ Mai Tai cocktail.

NOTES

[1] We prefer Myers's® Original Dark Rum for this cocktail.

[2] 10 Cane® is our preferred gold rum. Kirkland® Spiced Rum, Bacardi® and several others also work well.

[3] Use the amended version of Paul Clarke's #9 falernum recipe found in Appendix One.

MANHATTAN

The Manhattan is one of those old classics seen consumed in many of the great movies of the 1940s–1960s. It dropped out of favor for a while but, with the arrival of Don Draper and the *Mad Men* television series, emerged again in full force. This cocktail is a classic for good reason. Our Damn Near Perfect™ Manhattan is fairly traditional, except we find the use of Canadian whiskey to give a great balance that some other whiskeys lack.

- 2 oz. whiskey[1]
- 1 oz. sweet vermouth[2]
- ⅛ tsp. Angostura® bitters
- 1 cocktail cherry[3]
- 1 strip of lemon peel (about ⅛-inch wide)—all the white pith cut out

1. Fill a mixing glass with 3 or 4 ice cubes and let chill for a few minutes.
2. Pour the whiskey, vermouth, and bitters into the mixing glass and stir for a minute or so to chill it well.
3. Strain the mixture into a small Martini glass (or a nice Sherry glass), garnish with the cherry, and squeeze the lemon peel over the cocktail before hanging it on the rim or dropping it in.

The above measures yield **one** DNP™ Manhattan cocktail.

NOTES

[1] We prefer Pendleton Midnight slightly to Crown Royal® Canadian whiskey. Courvoisier® VSOP Cognac, Jack Daniels®, and Canadian Club® also make fine Manhattans.

[2] We prefer Noilly Prat® Rouge. Do not use ½ oz. sweet and ½ oz. dry vermouth.

[3] We prefer Bada Bing Cherries®.

MARGARITA FAMILY

Margaritas, in general, are among our most treasured cocktails. They come in many versions, ranging from those that are euphoric to absolutely terrible. Some Margarita recipes use blanco tequila (the least refined and aged), some use reposado (the intermediate tequila), and others use añejo (the most refined and aged). We do not use añejo in our cocktails because we believe the other two make better, more balanced, cocktails. We love añejo but limit its use to sipping it with just a couple drops of water added. Be sure to use 100-percent agave tequila—whichever brand and age you like.

S.

MARGARITA–BASIC

A simple, basic Margarita is a delightful cocktail when well made. The following is a standard recipe. Using fresh-squeezed lime juice and 100% agave tequila are the keys to great Margaritas.

- Kosher salt
- Lime wedge and slice
- ¼ cup tequila blanco (100% agave)[1]
- ½ Tbs. agave syrup OR 1 Tbs. prickly pear syrup OR 1 Tbs simple syrup
- 1½ Tbs. freshly squeezed lime juice

1. Pour salt on a small plate.
2. Rub lime wedge around the rim of a lowball, small Martini, or Sherry glass. Dip lime juice-rubbed rim into salt to coat—coating only half the rim allows sips from both salted and unsalted areas.
3. Put tequila, agave syrup, and lime juice into a cocktail shaker with ice cubes and shake vigorously about 30 to 40 times. Strain into salt-coated glass.
4. Add 1 or 2 ice cubes if you prefer to thin the cocktail a bit (Elaine prefers; I do not).
5. Garnish with lime slice.

The above measures yield **one** DNP™ Basic Margarita cocktail.

NOTES

[1] Best is the inexpensive 100 Anos blanco Kirkland® brand from Costco. It is excellent, as are many other 100-percent agave blanco tequilas.

MARGARITA–HOT SHOT

The Hot Shot is a fun, zippy Margarita. We tested it using ginger syrup as well as the version below and have a slight preference for the version below. The habanero hot sauce has a distinctive flavor, can be precisely measured, and keeps for months in a refrigerator.

- 3 thin slices of orange (juice orange, preferably)
- 1½ to 2 drops green habanero hot sauce, bottle well shaken[1]
- ½ Tbs. agave syrup
- 2 oz. reposado tequila[2]
- 1 oz. fresh squeezed lime juice
- ¼ tsp. Grand Marnier®
- Lime slice

1. Combine two of the three orange slices, habanero sauce drops, and agave syrup in a small mixing glass and muddle well.
2. Strain into a cocktail shaker, pressing down on the solids to extract as much liquid as possible.
3. Add tequila, lime juice, and Grand Marnier® to shaker, along with 5 or 6 ice cubes and shake vigorously (about 30 to 40 times).
4. Pour into a lowball glass and add 2 or 3 fresh ice cubes.
5. Garnish with one orange slice and one lime slice.

The above measures yield **one** DNP™ Hot Shot Margarita cocktail.

NOTES

[1] We use "El Yucateco®" for our habanero sauce; we suspect others will do quite nicely as well.

[2] We prefer 100 Años Sauza® reposado tequila, followed by 1800® reposado.

MARGARITA–PALOMA PICANTE

Paloma Margaritas stray from the more traditional ones by using grapefruit juice (or, in some cases, soft drinks such as "Squirt" that mimic the grapefruit taste). Many Paloma Margaritas do not use "heat." We like this DNP™ version because the habanero sauce complements the other tastes waltzing around in the cocktail.

- 2 oz. tequila blanco (100% agave)[1]
- 2 drops green habanero sauce[2]
- 2 oz. fresh-squeezed pink grapefruit juice (or Jarritos's™ Toronja (grapefruit juice)
- ½ oz. lime juice
- ½ oz. 1:1 simple syrup (1 cup sugar to 1 cup water)
- Very small pinch of salt (3 or 4 grains)
- 1½ oz. club soda
- Wedge of lime for garnish

1. In a shaker filled with ice, shake first six ingredients about 40 times.
2. Strain into a lowball glass with three ice cubes.
3. Pour in up to 1½ oz. of club soda.
4. Garnish with a lime wedge on the rim of the glass.

The above measures yield **one** DNP™ Paloma Picante cocktail.

NOTES

[1] We like Costco's Kirkland® tequila blanco (100% agave); many others will do well also.

[2] We use "El Yucateco®" habanero sauce; we suspect many others will work.

MARGARITA–TOP SHELF

We thank Rick Bayless for inspiring our "Top Shelf" version of this Margarita, which is slightly modified from his version. Although the 1800® reposado tequila he suggests leads to a wonderful result, our testing has convinced us that using 100 Años Sauza® reposado elevates the cocktail even higher. The virtues of this recipe are that it is beautifully balanced, can be made in advance, and quantities can be made to serve a lot of people—making it a perfect Margarita for cocktail parties. It's truly outstanding!

- 1⅔ cup reposado tequila[1]
- ¼ cup orange liqueur[2]
- ½ cup plus 1 Tbs. fresh-squeezed lime juice
- Zest from two medium limes (about 2 tsp.)
- 1 cup water
- 3 Tbs. sugar
- Lime wedges
- Kosher salt

1. Mix top four ingredients and set aside.
2. Make syrup by putting water and sugar in a pan and bringing to a boil. Cool completely and add to ingredients in Step 1.
3. Refrigerate in a jar with plastic wrap between lid and jar for 12 hours, shaking every few hours.
4. Strain through cheesecloth into a clean pitcher.
5. Rim five 5-oz. Martini glasses with salt, using lime juice on rim.
6. Refrigerate glasses.
7. Serve straight up or over ice in the prepared glasses.

The above measures yield **five** 5-oz. DNP™ cocktails.

NOTES

[1] We prefer 100 Años Sauza® reposado tequila.

[2] We like Torres's Gran Torres® Orange Liqueur or Magdala®. One can use Grand Marnier® or other orange-flavored liqueurs instead, but the elegance of this cocktail will suffer.

MARTINI FAMILY

The Martini is the epitome of a "cocktail." It is likely the best known of all cocktails, and it is certainly among the most controversial in terms of personal preferences. In addition to the classic Gin Martini and the classic Vodka Martini, there are many variations on those two themes as well as a host of new Martinis available in bars and restaurants (many having almost no resemblance to the classic versions).

The three Damn Near Perfect® Martinis on the following pages are ones we have spent hours testing. We have not tried all gin and vodka brands, or all possible proportions. Rather, we blind tested a wide assortment of ingredients and several proportions of ingredients.

If you prefer an olive garnish instead of a lemon, or no garnish, the difference between various brands of gin or vodka is somewhat muted (due to the powerful taste of the olive). Hence, the brand of gin or vodka is less important when ordering or making a Martini with an olive garnish.

Our classic Gin Martini and Vodka Martini each contain a bit of dry vermouth—which would horrify some who claim to imbibe Martinis when they, in some cases, are imbibing nothing but highly chilled glasses of gin or vodka. We believe for a cocktail to be called a Martini it must have at least some dry vermouth in it. That's our personal view—we believe it makes for the tastiest Martini. Our version of the Vesper Martini does not contain vermouth because it contains another ingredient of similar ilk.

Our thanks to Phil Eckhert, our fabulous photographer, for introducing us to the Vesper Martini.

MARTINI–ESPRESSO

The Espresso Martini below is a delicious version of this cocktail. It can be served early in the day as a "wake you up" cocktail—as long as you're not driving soon—or after dinner (if you don't mind the caffeine keeping you up a bit later than usual).

- 1¾ oz. vodka[1]
- 3 drops vanilla extract
- 1 oz. Bailey's®
- 1 oz. Kahlua™
- 1¾ oz. espresso coffee[2]
- 2 coffee beans

1. Put all liquid ingredients into a cocktail shaker with ice cubes. Shake 40 times.
2. Pour into a Martini glass that has about 2 Tbs. of crushed ice in it.
3. Carefully place coffee beans on top.

The above measures yield **one** DNP™ Espresso Martini.

NOTES

[1] We like Smirnoff #21™.

[2] Our Jura™ E8 espresso machine makes great espresso and does so easily.

MARTINI: GIN

The Gin Martini is, according to many, the "cocktail of cocktails." It is simple in terms of ingredients, easy to make, and wonderful when made well. With it come the usual Martini controversies: (1) whether to use vermouth; (2) whether to garnish with olive or lemon twist; and (3) which brand of gin to use.

If you are in Scotland or nearby, try the Isle of Bute Oyster® gin for a real treat! For this Martini, we rub half of the glass rim with lime and dip it on a plate with seaweed salt. Saltverk seaweed salt works well.

- 2 oz. English gin[1]
- ½ tsp. French dry vermouth
- Either one olive on a toothpick (our favorites are anchovy-stuffed olives), or a thin lemon twist (with pith removed) as garnish[2]

1. Chill the Martini glass in the freezer for ten minutes or longer before mixing cocktail. If time does not permit, fill the glass with crushed ice and let it sit for a couple of minutes to thoroughly chill it.

2. Fill a cocktail shaker with 5 or 6 ice cubes and pour in the gin and vermouth. Shake vigorously 40 times or so. Set the shaker down and let it sit for 30 seconds.

3. We like to place 2 or 3 small pieces of fresh crushed ice in the Martini glass (a practice that would be declared "heathen" by some) and then pour the mixture from the shaker into the glass—getting every drop out.

4. Garnish with an olive or lemon twist—whichever you prefer. If a lemon twist, squeeze over the cocktail before dropping it in the glass.

The above measures yield **one** DNP™ cocktail.

[1] For the lemon garnish version, we prefer Beefeater® gin AND Bombay Sapphire®; for the olive garnish version, we prefer Bombay Sapphire® gin followed by Beefeater®. All gins go well with anchovy-stuffed olives.

[2] Whether you use an olive or a lemon twist will greatly influence the flavor and texture of the cocktail. Elaine prefers the olive; I prefer the lemon twist. This cocktail can be ruined completely if the lemon strip is larger than ⅛-inch wide by 1-inch long.

MARTINI: VESPER

It is believed this cocktail was invented (or at least first reported) by Ian Fleming when he put it in the mouth of James Bond in his 1953 novel, *Casino Royale*. There, Bond named it in honor of Vesper Lynd, one of Fleming's dazzling female characters who was born on a "dark and stormy night." We've replaced Bond's instruction to use Lillet® with our own to use Cocchi® Americano Vermouth. In a sense, the Vesper is a hybrid between the gin Martini and the vodka Martini as it contains both of those liquors. Thanks to our outstanding photographer, Phil Eckhert, for introducing us to this cocktail.

- 1½ oz. English gin[1]
- 1 oz. vodka[2]
- ¼ to ½ oz. Cocchi® Americano or a dry Vermouth[3]
- Add a thin lemon twist (with pith removed) as garnish® (anchovy-stuffed olives are also excellent in this cocktail).[4]

1. Preferably, chill the Martini glass in the freezer for at least ten minutes before mixing the cocktail. If time does not permit, fill the glass with crushed ice and let it sit for a couple of minutes to thoroughly chill it.
2. Fill a cocktail shaker with 5 or 6 ice cubes.
3. Pour in the gin, vodka, and Cocchi® Americano or dry Vermouth.
4. Shake vigorously 40 times or so.
5. Set the shaker down and let it sit for 30 sec.
6. We like to place 2 or 3 small pieces of fresh crushed ice in the Martini glass (a practice that would be declared "heathen" by some) and then pour the mixture from the shaker into the glass—getting every drop out.
7. Garnish with the lemon twist, squeezing over the cocktail before dropping in the glass.

The above measures yield **one** DNP ™ cocktail.

[1] We prefer Beefeater® gin, closely followed by Bombay Sapphire®.

[2] We prefer Smirnoff® #21 Red Label.

[3] Dolin® is a great vermouth.

[4] This cocktail can be ruined completely if too large of a lemon strip is used. Do not exceed ⅛-inch wide by 1-inch long.

MARTINI–VODKA

The vodka Martini (or, as it is sometimes called, the "vodkatini") is a Martini that has stripped out the juniper flavors associated with most gin Martinis. It has the same elegance as a gin Martini and yet a totally different taste. We like both the gin and the vodka Martini, depending on our mood, and certainly recommend you try the DNP™ Vodka Martini below if you have avoided Vodka Martinis in the past.

- 3 oz. vodka[1]
- ½ tsp. French dry vermouth
- A thin, small lemon twist (with pith removed) as garnish[2]

1. Chill the Martini glass in the freezer for at least ten minutes before mixing the cocktail. If time does not permit, fill the glass with crushed ice and let it sit for a couple of minutes to thoroughly chill it.

2. Fill a cocktail shaker with 5 or 6 ice cubes and pour in the vodka and vermouth. Shake vigorously 40 times or so. Set the shaker down and let it sit for 30 seconds.

3. We like to place 2 or 3 small pieces of fresh crushed ice in the Martini glass (a practice that would be declared "heathen" by some) and then pour the mixture from the shaker into the glass, getting every drop out.

4. Garnish with the lemon twist, squeezing it over the cocktail before dropping it in the glass.

The above measures yield **one** DNP™ cocktail.

NOTES

[1] We prefer Smirnoff® #21 Red Label vodka.

[2] This cocktail can be ruined completely if the lemon strip is too large. Do not exceed ⅛-inch wide by 1-inch long.

MINT JULEP

No one should watch the Kentucky Derby without having a mint julep in hand! And yet, there are so many versions of this cocktail that it took years for us to find what we believe is the best one. And, for that, we are most grateful to David Embury and his excellent classic work, *The Fine Art of Mixing Drinks* (the second edition I have was published in 1952). Our version below of the mint julep is based on his sound advice.

- 1 8-oz. metal julep cup (as shown in the photo)
- 1 Tbs. 1:1 simple syrup
- 3 dashes Angostura bitters
- 2+ oz. bourbon[1]
- 12 tender, *smallish* mint leaves
- 1 large sprig mint with long stem

- Powdered sugar
- Lots of crushed ice (not slivers—blend in food processor to *really* crush it fine).

1. Put julep cup in a freezer for at least 10 min.
2. Wash large sprig of mint, dry almost completely, and dip in powdered sugar to coat the leaves. Set aside.
3. Put small mint leaves, simple syrup, and Angostura bitters in a mixing glass and muddle lightly with the mint on the glass bottom so the mint leaves are not crushed. Stir the mix.
4. Remove cup from freezer and fill completely with crushed ice. Strain mint mixture into cup over the ice.
5. Add 2 oz. of bourbon. Use a cocktail spoon to churn the ingredients up and down for a few minutes.
6. Add more ice—to the top.
7. Pour additional bourbon until ¼-inch from top.
8. Churn again with a spoon. Snip end of mint sprig stem and insert into cocktail with a straw cut to 6 inches.

The above measures yield **one** DNP™ Mint Julep.

NOTES

[1] We really like Evan Williams™ Single Barrel in this cocktail but it's difficult to find at retail. You may have to play around with a variety of bourbons to find the one you like best.

MOJITO

The Mojito is a national Cuban treasure. Rumored to have helped stave off scurvy in early sailing days, one can imagine the justifications for its frequent consumption. Our DNP™ Mojito follows the classic recipe for Mojitos, though for nice variations, you can substitute ginger syrup or St. Germain® for the simple syrup.

- 12 fresh mint leaves (fairly good-sized ones)
- ¾ oz. fresh lime juice
- ¾ oz. 1:1 simple syrup (1 cup sugar to 1 cup water)
- 3 oz. white rum[1]
- 2 to 3 oz. club soda (well chilled)
- Large sprig of fresh mint for garnish

1. In a tall, thin Collins glass (or a shorter, wide glass), gently muddle the mint leaves and the lime juice.[2]
2. Add the simple syrup
3. Top with 5 or 6 ice cubes.
4. Add the rum.
5. Add 2 to 3 oz. of club soda.
6. Stir, then serve with a straw (optional) and top with the sprig of fresh mint.

The above measures yield **one** DNP™ Mojito cocktail.

NOTES

[1] This drink is best with Havana Club 3-year-old rum. Bacardi™ works well too.

[2] Muddling too vigorously will release flavors that are too tart.

MONTE CARLO

The Monte Carlo is a simple cocktail to make and is extremely tasty with tequila, rum, or whiskey. We enjoy it with each of the whiskey choices. Our favorite is the rum version. And the Benedictine adds a nice touch. I'd like to dedicate this cocktail (even though I did not invent it) to John Rimarcik, who was a neighbor, good friend, and owner of the wonderful Monte Carlo restaurant in Minneapolis for many years. Before John passed away, he encouraged me to pursue the Damn Near Perfect® venture. Cheers to you, John!

- 2½ oz. good aged (añejo) tequila[1], or a good bourbon[2], or a good aged rum[3]
- ½ oz. Benedictine
- ⅛ tsp. Angostura bitters

1. Stir all ingredients in a large glass with large ice cubes for 30 seconds. Pour into a lowball glass over fresh ice.

The above measures yield **one** DNP™ Monte Carlo cocktail.

NOTES

[1] Sauza™ Conmemorativo tequila is excellent.

[2] We like Michter's Kentucky Straight Bourbon™, and Evan Williams™ Single Barrel bourbon (which is difficult to find these days).

[3] Metusalem™ Gran Reserve is an excellent rum for this cocktail.

MY, YER WONDERFUL!

This is a beautifully balanced cocktail. It is named after my good friend Jeff Meyer (aka: Spider) because he loves the cocktail and he's "wonderful!" The combination of the Meyer lemon juice and the egg white make for a scrumptious DNP™ cocktail—one of our very favorites! Make the rim coating well in advance of consumption.

- 5 or 6 Meyer lemons, zested and halved, yielding 4 to 5 tsp. with 1½ tsp. of zest
- 1 Tbs. sugar
- ½ tsp. Kosher salt
- ¾ oz. fresh squeezed Meyer lemon juice (from the previously zested halves)
- 1 oz. Citroen vodka[1]
- 1 oz. plain vodka (in addition to the Citroen vodka)[2]
- ½ oz. elderflower syrup[3]
- 1 egg white —we recommend pasteurized

1. Zest the lemon with a Microplane®. Press on paper towels to extract as much moisture as possible. Do this a couple of times and let it air dry for an hour or so. Chop dried zest as fine as possible so it's almost like dust. You should end up with about ¼ tsp. of this final mixture for each of the 5 or 6 lemons you zest. Mix with the sugar and salt. Make lots of it; it keeps almost indefinitely in a glass jar.
2. Moisten a small Martini-shaped glass rim with water and rim the glass with above mixture.
3. Squeeze the zested lemon to extract the ¾ oz. of juice.
4. Put lemon juice, the two vodkas, and elderflower syrup in a prep glass.

5. Put egg white in a coffee mug and whip with a hand immersion[4] blender until frothy. If only making one cocktail, you may need two egg whites to have enough for the mixer blade to reach the egg whites.

6. Fill a cocktail shaker with about six ice cubes and pour in the whipped egg white, followed by the vodka/lemon juice/elderflower syrup mixture.

7. Pour a bit of the syrup mixture into the coffee mug to be sure all the egg white makes it to the shaker. Shake 30 to 40 times. Pour into the glass rimmed with the zest/salt/sugar mixture.

8. The above measures yield **one** DNP™ "My, Yer Wonderful" cocktail.

NOTES

[1] We prefer Ketel One Citroen® vodka

[2] We like Smirnoff® #21 Red label for the regular vodka.

[3] We prefer d'Arbo® syrup because it is less sweet than some others (e.g., St. Germain®) and can easily be purchased online.

[4] If you do not have an immersion blender you can get decent foam by extensive heavy shaking (or by doing the "dry shake"). The immersion blender works better, though.

NEGRONI—NONTRADITIONAL

This cocktail is a wonderful alternative to the classic Negroni, which many people find to be too bitter (with its use of Campari™). Substituting Aperol™ for the Campari™ tones it down a bit and results in a real favorite. The recipe for the Negroni (either style) is easy to remember: The alcohol is 1:1:1.

- 1 oz. Aperol™
- 1 oz. gin[1]
- 1 oz. sweet Vermouth[2]
- 2 drops orange bitters
- ½ orange slice for garnish

1. Fill mixing glass with ice to chill.
2. Add Aperol™, gin, sweet vermouth, and orange bitters. Stir hard for 30 seconds.
3. Strain into a chilled cocktail glass; hang orange peel or drop it into cocktail.

The above measures yield **one** DNP™ non-traditional Negroni cocktail.

NOTES

[1] Gordon's™ gin works well and is inexpensive.

[2] Cocci di Torino™ is a reliable sweet vermouth.

NORMANDY

This is a standard cocktail in the Normandy area of France. As with many other DNP™ cocktails, we much prefer using Meyer lemon to keep the acidity manageable. And a high-quality Calvados is essential.

- 9 fresh cranberries[1]
- 3 slices of Granny Smith apple, each cut in half
- 1 tsp. dark brown sugar
- ½ oz. lemon juice (preferably from a Meyer lemon)
- 1½ tsp 1:1 dark brown sugar simple syrup (1 cup brown sugar to 1 cup water)
- ¼ cup good quality Calvados[2]

1. Muddle 6 cranberries, 4 half slices of apple, and the brown sugar in a short glass.
2. Add the lemon juice, brown sugar syrup, and the Calvados.
3. Put about 12 ice cubes in a cocktail shaker, add mixture, and shake 40 to 50 times.
4. Pour into strainer and through funnel, pushing down with the back of the spoon to extract juices. Strain into 8 or 9 oz. lowball glass with 5 or 6 ice cubes (do not use one large cube!).
5. Put 3 nice dark red cranberries on a skewer and center the skewer over the cocktail.

The above measures yield **one** DNP™ Normandy cocktail.

NOTES

[1] In a pinch, frozen cranberries that have been thoroughly thawed can be used instead of fresh ones.

[2] We like Calvados™ Boulard and Calvados du Pays d'Auge Reserve.

OARSMAN

The Oarsman cocktail is especially delightful on a hot summer day. The juices needed can be found in Mexican grocery stores and other stores with a wide variety of juices.

- ¼ cup papaya juice, nectar, or mango juice[1]
- ¼ cup cranberry juice cocktail[2]
- 1½ oz. rum[3]
- $1/16$ tsp. coconut extract
- 1 oz. Cointreau
- ¾ cup crushed ice (per cocktail)

1. Put all ingredients into a blender and briefly pulse a few times to get a slushy mixture that is frothy on top. Don't overdo it.
2. Serve in a stemmed glass.

The above measures yield **one** DNP™ Oarsman cocktail.

NOTES

[1] Goya™ and Jumex™ are good brand choices.

[2] We like Ocean Spray Cranberry Juice Cocktail.

[3] Myers's™ Original Dark Rum is an excellent choice!

OAXACA MAGNÍFICO

This cocktail is a nice twist on many other stirred cocktails, highlighting tequila and the smoky taste of mescal. Some people prefer various other bitters to Angostura® (e.g., Xocolatl Mole™ bitters) for this cocktail, but our blind tasting with discerning friends Joe Dowling and Siobhan Cleary convinced us that Angostura® excels here.

- 1½ oz. reposado tequila[1]
- ½ oz. mescal[2]
- ½ tsp. elderflower syrup[3]
- ¼ tsp. Angostura® bitters, or Bittermens® Xocolatl Mole™ bitters
- Strip of orange peel with pith removed

1. Chill a mixing glass and a lowball glass in the freezer.
2. Stir first four ingredients with ice in the mixing glass, stirring until very cold. Strain into a chilled lowball glass with 2 or 3 fresh ice cubes.
3. Twist orange peel over the drink and drop it into the cocktail.

The above measures yield **one** DNP™ Oaxaca Magnífico cocktail.

NOTES

[1] Use either 1800® or 100 Años Sauza® tequila.

[2] Sacrificio® reposado is the safest bet for mescal as some others (e.g., Scorpion® and Monte Alban®) are too smoky for this drink.

[3] We prefer d'Arbo® syrup because it is less sweet than some others and can easily be purchased online.

OLD FASHIONED—MAPLE

This is a wonderful, simple version of an Old Fashioned that I only recently discovered. The maple syrup adds a great taste that makes this a superlative before-bedtime cocktail.

- 2 oz. bourbon[1] or rye whiskey[2]
- ¼ oz. (½ Tbs) maple syrup (room temperature so it can be stirred in)
- 3 dashes orange bitters
- Orange twist
- Freshly grated nutmeg

1. Put all liquid ingredients (first three in list) in an Old Fashioned glass with one large ice cube. Stir until well chilled.
2. Garnish with orange twist and sprinkle freshly grated nutmeg over the top.

The above measures yield **one** DNP™ Maple Old Fashioned cocktail.

NOTES

[1] Our bourbon preferences for this cocktail are Michter's Small Batch Kentucky Straight Bourbon™, Evan Williams Single Barrel®, and Buffalo Trace™.

[2] We really like Michter's™ Single Barrel Kentucky Straight Rye for the rye whiskey.

OLD FASHIONED–RIGHT PLACE, RIGHT THYME

This is a variation on the Maple Old Fashioned cocktail. The slight differences between these two cocktails do make a real tasty difference, and it's worth trying them both.

- 2 oz. rye bourbon[1] or rye whiskey[2]
- 1½ tsp. maple syrup
- ⅛ tsp. Angostura bitters
- Lemon peel
- Thyme sprig

1. Combine whiskey, maple syrup, and bitters into an iced shaker and stir for ten seconds.
2. Pour into a rocks glass over a large ice cube. Squeeze lemon peel over the beverage.
3. Garnish with the thyme sprig and the lemon peel.

The above measures yield **one** DNP™ Old Fashioned–Right Place, Right Thyme cocktail.

NOTES

[1] We really like Michter's™ Small Batch Kentucky Straight Bourbon whiskey.

[2] Michter's™ Single Barrel Straight Rye is also excellent for this cocktail.

OLD FASHIONED–TRADITIONAL

What can you say? Along with the Martini, the Old Fashioned is another classic cocktail making a strong comeback. Most bartenders have their favorite version among the dozens of recipes. We think our version is Damn Near Perfect®.

OPTION 1

- ¼ oz. demerara syrup, made with equal amounts of demerara sugar and water
- ¼ oz. white syrup made with equal amounts of regular white sugar and water
- 5 drops (no more!) Angostura® bitters
- 5 drops cherry bitters
- 1½ orange slices
- 2 cocktail cherries[1]
- Splash of club soda (about ½ oz.)
- 2 oz. whiskey (1 oz. rye whiskey[2] and 1 oz. bourbon[3])

OPTION 2

- Instead of two syrups, using ½ oz. of Piloncello syrup (Earl Giles™ brand) yields an excellent result!

1. In the bottom of a short glass, muddle the syrup, bitters, 1 orange slice, 1 of the 2 cherries, and the ½ oz. of club soda.

2. Remove the fruit husks, or strain into a 6-oz. (when full) Old Fashioned lowball glass, pressing down on the husks to get the juice out. Discard the husks.

3. Add the whiskeys and three ice cubes. Stir.

4. Garnish with the remaining one-half orange slice, dropping it into the glass with the remaining cherry set on top of it.

The above measures yield **one** DNP™ Old Fashioned cocktail.

NOTES

[1] We prefer Bada Bing Cherries® to maraschino.

[2] Our preference is Michter's™ Single Barrel Kentucky Straight Rye.

[3] Our bourbon preferences for an Old Fashioned are Michter's™ Small Batch Kentucky Straight Bourbon, Buffalo Trace™, and Evan Williams Single Barrel® (which is very hard to find).

PISCO SOUR

Chileans and Peruvians have fought for years over who invented the Pisco Sour and whether it should be made in the Chilean or Peruvian manner. Having traveled to both countries and sampled extensively, we opt for the Chilean version. One reason is the difficulty of obtaining mild Peruvian Pisco in the US.

- 1 egg white (3 Tbs.) —we recommend pasteurized
- 2 oz. Chilean Pisco[1]
- ½ oz. fresh squeezed lime juice
- ¾ oz. 1:1 simple syrup (1 cup sugar to 1 cup water)
- 3 drops Angostura® bitter

1. Dry shake by putting all ingredients in a cocktail shaker, tightly sealing it, and shaking for 20 seconds to foam the egg white. Or put the egg white into a coffee mug and use a hand immersion blender to blend until frothy[2].

2. If using an immersion blender, afterwards pour mixture into cocktail shaker. Fill shaker with ice and shake 40 times.

3. Strain into Old Fashioned glass (or small Martini glass) without ice. Be sure to scoop some foam into the glass.

4. Put 3 drops of Angostura® bitters on top and drag a toothpick across the bitters to form a nice design. Serve.

The above measures yield **one** DNP™ Pisco Sour cocktail.

[1] The best Chilean piscos we've been able to easily find in the U.S. are Alto del Carmen® and Capel®. If you are in Chile, order Horcon Quemado® 40 (80 proof). Or, if you find a way to obtain Horcon Quemado® in the U.S., please let us know how to do so. It is supreme!

[2] If only making one cocktail, you may need to use two egg whites to attain enough depth for the mixer blades to do their job. This bit of extra egg white will not harm the cocktail. If you do not have an immersion blender, you can still get decent foam by extensive and heavy shaking. The immersion blender works better though.

PISCO SOUR WITH GUAVA

This variation of the basic Pisco Sour contains guava syrup that adds a tasty touch. The method described in Step 1 is the dry-shake method used by bartenders to obtain sufficient foam from the egg white.

- 2 oz. Chilean Pisco[1]
- ½ oz. fresh squeezed lime juice
- ¾ oz. guava syrup[2]
- 1 egg white (3 Tbs.)[3] —we recommend pasteurized
- 2 to 5 drops Angostura® bitters

1. Dry shake by putting all ingredients in a cocktail shaker, sealing and shaking for 20 seconds to foam the egg white. *Alternatively*, put the egg white into a coffee mug and use a hand immersion blender to blend until frothy. Then add to the cocktail shaker.

2. Add 3 or 4 ice cubes to the cocktail shaker and shake 30 to 40 times.

3. Carefully remove the ice cubes from the shaker and pour mixture into chilled Old Fashioned (or small Martini) glass—without ice. Be sure to scoop some foam on top of the liquid in the glass.

4. 4. Add 3 drops of Angostura® bitters on top and drag a toothpick across the bitters to form a nice design. Serve.

The above measures yield **one** DNP™ Pisco Sour with Guava cocktail.

NOTES

[1] The best Chilean Piscos we've been able to find easily in the U.S. are Alto del Carmen® and Capel®. If you are in Chile, order Horcon Quemado® 40 (80 proof). Or, if you find a way to obtain Horcon Quemado® in the U.S., please let us know how to do so. It is supreme!

[2] Torani™ brand is an excellent guava syrup for this cocktail.

[3] If making one cocktail with immersion blender, you may need two egg whites to attain enough depth for the mixer blades. Extra egg white will not harm the cocktail. If you do not have an immersion blender, you can still get decent foam by extensive heavy shaking. The immersion blender works better though.

PLANTER'S PUNCH

This is one of the "oldie but goodie" rum drinks. Some say it originated in South Carolina's Planters Inn. Others say Jamaica. It's often too sweet and we have adjusted ours to where we feel it's a most refreshing and rewarding DNP™ cocktail.

- 1 oz. white rum
- ¾ oz. grenadine[1]
- 1½ oz. fresh squeezed pineapple juice
- 2 oz. fresh squeezed orange juice
- ¼ oz. fresh squeezed lemon juice
- ½ oz. fresh squeezed grapefruit juice[2]
- ½ oz. dark rum[3]
- Orange slice and cocktail cherry[4] as garnishes

1. Fill a tall cocktail glass with ice and pour in first six ingredients.
2. Stir.
3. Float the dark rum on top
4. Garnish with an orange slice and cherry.
5. Serve with a straw.

The above measures yield **one** DNP™ Planter's Punch cocktail.

NOTES

[1] Preferably use homemade grenadine (see Appendix One). If using commercial grenadine, you may wish to cut it back to ½ oz.

[2] Ruby Red grapefruit is preferable.

[3] We prefer Myers's® Original Dark Rum.

[4] We prefer Bada Bing Cherries® to maraschino cherries.

RAMOS GIN FIZZ

Elaine has perfected this New Orleans classic through long-term tinkering. The keys are to let the blender run for the full two minutes. Do not add the lemon juice until you have started the blending or the cocktail will curdle. This refreshing cocktail is a great way to use leftover egg whites you may have from the last time you used yolks to make a crème brulée. If tripling the recipe, to have enough for refills for two, re-blend for an additional 30 seconds or so before pouring the leftovers into the glasses of your eagerly awaiting guests.

- 1½ oz. gin[1]
- 2 drops orange flower water
- 1 egg white —we recommend pasteurized
- 2½ tsp. confectioner's (powdered) sugar[2]
- 2 oz. half and half[3]
- 1 or 2 drops vanilla extract
- ½ cup ice cubes
- 1 small squeeze lemon juice (⅓ tsp.)
- Nutmeg, cut in half, ready to rub across a Microplane®

1. Combine gin, orange flower water, egg white, confectioner's sugar, half and half, vanilla extract, and ice in blender and blend on high speed for two minutes, adding the squeeze of lemon juice after a few seconds (not before).
2. Pour into a tall, thin glass or beer glass; sprinkle with nutmeg that's been rubbed over a Microplane®.

The above measures yield **one** DNP™ Ramos Gin Fizz cocktail served in a tall, thin glass.

NOTES

[1] We prefer Bombay Sapphire® gin or Tanqueray gin®. Some other English gins contain too much juniper

[2] If doubling, use 4½ tsp.; if tripling, use 7 tsp.

[3] Do not use heavy cream.alternative.

ROB ROY

This cocktail is, in some sense, thought of as a variation of the Old Fashioned, though I don't think of it in quite that way. It varies quite a bit depending on the Scotch that is used—not only the brand but the age of the Scotch. Ellis, the bartender at the Waldorf Astoria Caledonian Hotel in Edinburgh was very helpful in guiding me through several recipes for this cocktail.

- 1¾ oz. Scotch[1]
- ¾ oz. Cocchi Storico Vermouth di Torino (sweet)
- 4 drops Angostura bitters
- 1 orange rind
- 2 cocktail cherries[2]

1. Fill Champagne glass completely with crushed ice and let sit 5 minutes to thoroughly chill the glass.
2. Put first three ingredients in a cocktail shaker with five ice cubes and stir for 10 seconds. Then shake.
3. Empty glass of crushed ice and wipe dry. Strain liquids into the glass.
4. Garnish with orange peel and two cherries on a stick. Serve.

The above measures yield **one** DNP™ Rob Roy cocktail.

ALTERNATIVE

A nice, simple alternative to try is to shake together 1½ oz. Dewar's Scotch, ½ oz. Punt e Mes Vermouth, and 2 dashes of Peychaud bitters.

NOTES

[1] Glenfiddich™ 14-year-old single barrel works very well as do, I'm sure, other high quality Scotch whiskeys.

[2] Bada Bing® cherries work well, as do many others.

RUM PUNCH

This is one of our favorite summertime rum-based Damn Near Perfect® cocktails. Fresh ingredients and Myers's® Original Dark Rum are critical to attain the proper balance and character.

- 1 oz. dark rum[1]
- 1 oz. light rum[2]
- 1 oz. fresh squeezed pineapple juice
- ¼ cup fresh squeezed orange juice
- Splash of fresh squeezed grapefruit juice[3]
- Splash of coconut-flavored rum
- Splash of grenadine[4]
- ⅛ tsp. 151-proof rum (optional)
- Orange slice and cocktail cherry as garnishes[5]

1. Fill a cocktail shaker halfway with ice cubes.
2. Add all ingredients except the optional 151-proof rum and garnishes.
3. Shake well 40 times or so.
4. Pour into well-chilled, large glass filled halfway with ice cubes.
5. Top with a float of the 151-proof rum, if desired.
6. Garnish with the orange slice and cocktail cherry.
7. Serve with a straw.

The above measures yield **one** DNP™ Rum Punch cocktail.

NOTES

[1] We strongly prefer Myers's® Original Dark Rum for this cocktail.

[2] Havana Club® made in Cuba is best for the light rum; maybe we'll be able to buy it in the U.S. soon! Otherwise, Bacardi® is fine.

[3] Preferably use Ruby Red grapefruit.

[4] Preferably use homemade grenadine; see Appendix One.

[5] We prefer Bada Bing Cherries™ to maraschino cherries.

SANGRIA

We count our recipe for Sangria as a cocktail because it contains Cointreau®. The recipe below is adapted from the one we believe was used at the Spanish Embassy in Washington, DC, some time ago. It's not overly sweet and we find it to be delightful for guest gatherings. You must use an inexpensive red wine—pricy reds ruin the Sangria!

- 2 large juice oranges, washed
- 1 lemon—washed and sliced
- ¼ cup sugar
- ¼ cup Cointreau®
- 1 750 ml. bottle of inexpensive fruity red wine[1]

1. Slice one orange and cut it in half; juice the other one.
2. Put the sliced orange, sliced lemon, and sugar in a large pitcher; mash gently until some juice is released and the sugar dissolves—about one minute.
3. Stir in orange juice, Cointreau®, and wine. Refrigerate for at least two hours—up to eight-plus hours is fine.
4. Before serving, add 6 to 8 ice cubes and stir briskly to distribute the settled fruit. Add an ice cube and a piece of fruit to each wine glass.

The above measures yield **four** DNP™ glasses of Sangria.

NOTES

[1] Confidencial™ is an excellent choice for the red wine, as is Sangre de Toro.

SAZERAC

The Sazerac is a classic New Orleans cocktail. Unfortunately, the exposure most tourists get to this cocktail is mediocre at best. Our DNP™ Sazerac evolved over about sixteen months of experimentation. Bradley, our wonderful bartender on our Crystal® *Symphony* cruise, proved to us the superiority of Jameson Irish Whiskey® as opposed to American rye whiskey. Further tinkering resulted in our use of an orange peel rather than the lemon peel so often used. Cold, cold, cold is critical; hence, take care to follow the temperature-related directions in steps 1 to 4 below.

- 1 tsp. 1:1 simple syrup (1 cup sugar to 1 cup water)
- ¼ tsp. Peychaud® bitters
- 2 oz. whiskey[1]
- Small amount of absinthe (about ⅛ tsp.)[2]
- 1½-inch x ¾-inch slice of orange peel—all pith scraped out

1. Fill an Old Fashioned lowball glass with crushed ice and let it sit to chill the glass.
2. Put a mixing glass in a freezer for about 10 minutes to thoroughly chill.
3. Take the chilled glass from the freezer and fill with ice cubes and the simple syrup, Peychaud® bitters, and whiskey. Stir well for several minutes to thoroughly chill mixture.
4. Empty the glass that contains crushed ice, pour about ⅛ tsp. of absinthe in it, and swirl around. Pour out absinthe (hopefully into another glass awaiting the next Sazerac!).
5. Re-stir the glass with the whiskey, and strain into the glass with absinthe coating.
6. Squeeze an orange piece over drink and drop in.

The above measures yield **one** DNP™ cocktail.

NOTES

[1] We prefer Jameson Irish Whiskey®.

[2] We use Absinthe 110®. Use Pernod® as an alternative..alternative.

SIDECAR

The Sidecar renaissance is here! It was in the early 1900s when the Ritz Hotel in Paris claims to have initiated it. Most people believe it was named after motorcycle sidecars and may have started toward the end of WWI. We thought ours was excellent until Bradley showed us how Courvoisier® elevates it. Later, we found that using Meyer lemons moves the Sidecar closer to perfection.

- ½ tsp. ground cinnamon
- 1 Tbs. superfine sugar
- 1½ oz. Cognac[1]
- ¾ oz. Cointreau®
- ½ oz. freshly squeezed lemon juice[2]
- Large ice sphere (one per glass if a wide Old Fashioned-style glass is used) or an ice cube (if a narrower Sherry-style glass is used)
- Strip of orange peel (½-inch wide, about 1-inch long)—pith removed

1. Shake the cinnamon-sugar mixture to combine.
2. Rim the glass with the wet pulp of the juiced lemon and dip into the cinnamon-sugar mixture so the outer rim of the glass is lightly coated. Chill glass in a freezer for 5 minutes (or longer).
3. Shake the Cognac, Cointreau®, and lemon juice in a cocktail shaker half full of ice cubes. Shake about 40 times.
4. Remove glass from freezer, add an ice sphere or ice cube, and strain cocktail ingredients from the shaker into the glass.
5. Garnish with the orange strip and serve.

The above measures yield **one** DNP™ Sidecar cocktail.

NOTES

[1] Courvoisier® VSOP is the best Cognac we've found for this cocktail; next is Remy Martin® VSOP.

[2] We have a strong preference for Meyer lemon juice for this cocktail. If Meyer lemons are not available, be careful to avoid using too much regular lemon juice. A good trick is to make lots of Meyer lemon juice and freeze it into 2 oz. cubes to be thawed and used for future cocktails.alternative.

SURF SIDER

The Surf Sider can be made in the blue (using blue Curaçao) or the green (using Midori™) style. They are totally different from each other—and we love them both!

- 1½ oz. white rum
- 1½ oz. pineapple juice (fresh is best, canned works in a pinch)
- ½ oz. fresh squeezed lemon juice
- ¾ oz. 2:1 simple syrup (2 cups water to 1 cup sugar)
- 1¼ cup crushed ice
- ¾ oz. Bols™ Blue Curaçao or Midori™—either works well

1. Put all ingredients in a blender and blend until smooth (use the pulse setting to make sure all ice lumps have dissolved).
2. Strain into either a tall glass or a Martini-style glass.
3. Serve with a straw if you wish.

The above measures yield **one** DNP™ Surf Sider cocktail.

THE 15TH HOLE

The 15th Hole is obviously named for golf aficionados. Although golf drinks are often called "The 19th Hole" because they are enjoyed in the clubhouse after the round, this is a refreshing cocktail that's especially appropriate at that point in one's golf round when things are not going well. The cocktail is quite different depending on the rum used.

- ¾ oz. fresh lime juice
- 1 oz. dark rum[1]
- 1 oz. blanco tequila
- ½ oz. Cointreau®
- 1 tsp. maraschino liqueur
- ¼ oz. agave syrup
- 1 dash orange bitters

1. Fill rocks glass with 4 or 5 ice cubes to chill (or put in a freezer for a while).
2. In a cocktail shaker, combine all ingredients and shake with ice cubes.
3. Put fresh ice cubes in the chilled glasses and pour the cocktail from the shaker into the glass.

The above measures yield **one** DNP™ The 15th Hole cocktail

NOTES

[1] Our preference is Myers's™ dark rum. Other rums provide nice variations. alternative.

APPENDIX ONE

FALERNUM SYRUP

Falernum is a special syrup heavily influenced by cloves. Debates rage as to whose falernum is superior. The one below is adapted from Paul Clarke's #9 (from "The Cocktail Chronicles"). We've chosen to make a simple syrup as noted in Step 3 rather than putting the sugar and water in a jar and shaking it to dissolve. Our tests show no discernible difference in how well the two methods work and no tastable difference in the result. As a side benefit, we have found that some test cocktails we would otherwise have thrown out can be salvaged by adding a bit of this falernum.

- 2 Tbs. blanched, slivered almonds
- 40 whole cloves
- ¾ cup white rum
- Finely grated zest of 9 medium limes with no pith at all (about 3½ Tbs.)
- One 3-inch piece of fresh ginger, peeled and julienned
- 1½ cups plus 2 Tbs. superfine sugar
- ¾ cup plus 1 Tbs. warm water
- 3 Tbs. fresh lime juice, strained
- ¼ tsp. almond extract

1. Toast almonds and cloves until almonds are golden and cloves are aromatic—about 5 minutes. Cool slightly off the heat, about 3 minutes.

2. Crush the cloves in a mortar. Then place almonds, crushed cloves, rum, lime zest, and ginger in a two-cup glass container with a tight-fitting lid (use plastic wrap between glass and lid). Cover, shake to combine, and let sit for 24 hours at room temperature.

3. Combine sugar and water in a small saucepan and bring to a boil while occasionally stirring. As soon as the mixture comes to a boil, give it a good quick stir and remove from the heat. Let it cool.

4. After 24 hours, strain the rum mixture through moistened cheesecloth set in a fine mesh strainer over a small bowl. Press solids to extract juice. Discard solids.

5. Add strained liquid, lime juice, and almond extract to the reserved simple syrup, then shake.

6. Keep refrigerated up to three months.

7. The above measures yield two to three cups of DNP™ Falernum syrup.

GRENADINE

Homemade grenadine syrup is easy to make and much nicer in DNP™ cocktails than the store-bought varieties. It's nothing more than a version of simple syrup except pomegranate juice is used instead of water.

- ¾ cup granulated sugar
- ¾ cup pomegranate juice[1]

1. Stir sugar into pomegranate juice and bring to a boil in a saucepan, stirring occasionally.
2. When boil is reached, give it a couple of good stirs to be sure the sugar is dissolved, remove from heat, and let cool. Yields about 1 cup.
3. Store in the refrigerator for several weeks (if it lasts that long) in a glass container with a piece of plastic wrap over it so it can be shaken before each use (though this may not be necessary).

The above measures yield 1 cup of grenadine.

NOTES

[1] *Must* be a pomegranate juice with no sugar having been added!

SIMPLE SYRUP

Simple syrup is a mainstay in many cocktails. It "simply" consists of combining a certain amount of water with a certain amount of sugar to create a syrup. The amount of syrup versus the amount of water can vary. When we specify a "1:1 syrup" it refers to a syrup made with equal amounts of water and sugar. Hence, a "2:1 syrup" refers to a syrup with twice as much water as sugar, so it is less sweet. It's fun to create other syrups around this basic recipe. Any amount can be made, but the syrup is so easy to make there is no reason to make more than you will need for a couple of weeks. It refrigerates well.

Tip: If a cocktail recipe calls for sugar itself, adding one-third more 1:1 simple syrup will yield a comparable result (e.g., use 1⅓ tsp. of 1:1 simple syrup in place of 1 tsp. of sugar). However, if the recipe calls for muddling with sugar, use sugar, as its coarseness helps the muddling process.

- ¾ cup granulated sugar
- ¾ cup water

1. Stir sugar into water and bring to a boil in a saucepan, stirring occasionally.
2. When boil is reached, give it a couple of good stirs to be sure the sugar is dissolved, remove from heat, and let cool.
3. Store in the refrigerator for several weeks.

SWEET 'N SOUR MIX

Most sweet 'n sour mixes we have purchased in bottles are, in a word, atrocious! We suspect the preservatives in them are mostly to blame. To make matters worse, many cocktails purchased in chain restaurants, and in some bars, include a sweet 'n sour mix they have bought from a liquor distributor and is equally horrible. This epidemic is so widespread that we will not purchase a Margarita in a restaurant until the server has given us a small sample to taste of any sweet 'n sour mix that is included in the cocktail. However, there is a simple remedy for this problem—make your own sweet 'n sour mix. It's very easy.

- 1 part lime juice[1]
- 1 part lemon juice
- 1 part 1:1 simple syrup
- 2 parts water

1. Put all ingredients in a glass jar, cover with a piece of plastic wrap, and shake until well mixed.
2. Use at once or refrigerate for up to three days. After that, the acids from the limes and lemons start to turn a bit.

NOTES

[1] For the juice, we prefer squeezing the smallish Mexican limes, not Key limes, as they are a tad less acerbic.

APPENDIX TWO

Scientific Method Used to Create
Damn Near Perfect® Cocktails

The scientific method seeks to eliminate biases from conclusions—or, at least, limit them as much as possible. Our method for doing so consists of the following:

- Start with a popular version of a cocktail and taste it.

- When we find this first version is too sweet, too sour, too strong, unbalanced, or "off" in some other way, we adjust the offending ingredient(s) until we feel the resulting cocktail is well balanced, which is the key to all great cocktails.

- We then blind test various brands that make up the cocktail. For example, if we are testing a Margarita, we test many versions using different brands (and types—e.g., blanco, reposado, etc.) of tequila. Test glasses are labeled with a Post-it™ on the bottom of the glass so we cannot tell when tasting which brand (or type) of tequila is in each glass, and the glasses are placed on the testing table by a person who did not mix them—further eliminating knowledge of the brand (or type) in each glass. Obviously, identical glassware is used, and the exact ingredient amounts are used for each so there are no visual cues as to the different ingredients. In cases where the colors of the tested ingredients vary, we close our eyes as the glasses are randomly placed on the table, then one of us gingerly moves them about, and we carefully grope for each so we don't knock them over.

- When there are many variables we wish to test (or many brands or types of ingredients), we go through many trials—sometimes testing two versions and other times testing three. We do not believe testing more than three cocktail versions at one time results in reliable results.

- Only when we reach a stage where Elaine and I agree the cocktail is better than all the others we have tasted, is that cocktail certified as DNP™.

- An example of how complex some of the testing can be is the testing for our Gin and Tonic—to which we have alluded earlier. Many things can be varied, including:
  - Gin brand
  - Tonic brand (and variations within a brand)
  - Ratio of gin to tonic (i.e., how much of each is poured in the glass)
  - Whether a lime or lemon is used as a garnish
  - Whether regular ice cubes are used (and how many) or tonic frozen in the shape of ice cubes is used (so the cocktail is not diluted as the ice melts).
- We started with the decision to use 2 ounces of gin, 5 ice cubes, and enough tonic to fill a standard Gin and Tonic tall glass (12-ounce capacity right to the top rim). Then we tested three gins at a time by making the identical cocktail for each but only varying the gin. This meant we used the same tonic, a lime, and regular ice cubes for each version. We tasted each and indicated our preferences. We repeated (on a different day) with three different gins and, on a subsequent day, we paired off the winners from the first two days of testing. At that point, we had our preferred order of gins.
- We followed by testing the preferred two gins against each of four tonics and selected the winners. (Interestingly, different gins won with different tonics.) Following that, we tested lemon vs. lime garnishes, then tonic vs. water ice cubes. (We know; it's arduous work, but someone has to do it!)

Those familiar with experimental design will recognize that with all these variables there are interaction effects (as noted above). The perfect gin, for example, can vary depending on how the other ingredients are combined. And a given Gin and Tonic may taste better on a very hot day than on a colder day. This is why our objective is Damn Near Perfect®, and not perfection. We will keep trying new configurations and adjusting as we go. We hope you will too. Let us know what you discover.

Important Learnings

Below are some important facts we have learned so far during our fun adventure:

- The most expensive liquor does not always produce the best result. Liquor prices are affected by the cost of production and distribution, the costs associated with marketing, and what consumers will pay for the brand name. Many great liquors do not incur high marketing costs and, therefore, are priced lower than their inferior competitors who spend heavily on marketing.

- The same brand of liquor may excel in one cocktail and be less spectacular in another. An example of this is our preference for Tanqueray® gin in our version of the Juliet and Romeo cocktail, whereas we do not believe Tanqueray® makes the best Gin Martini. The "sad" result of this finding is that to have on hand the capability to make a variety of DNP™ cocktails, you will need lots of space in which to store your extensive collection of liquor brands.

- The "best" type of liquor does not always make the best cocktail. For example, tequilas are aged to varying levels of "quality"—blanco, reposado, and añejo—with pricing following this hierarchy. While añejo tequilas may be superior for sipping by themselves, they often overpower certain cocktails, which are better balanced by either blanco or reposado tequilas. We prefer blanco (fortunately, the least expensive) tequila for Basic Margaritas, and we prefer reposado tequila for our Top Shelf version. This does not mean we have no añejo in our cupboard; we limit its use to sipping it by itself with just a drop or two of water.

- It's fun to play around with a wide variety of liquors and support ingredients. For example, you will notice we have recommended Meyer lemon juice in some of our cocktails as opposed to juice from traditional lemons. We do this because the juice of Meyer lemons is milder and more consistent in its strength. Regular store-bought lemons vary in terms of how strong they are, which makes it difficult to settle on an exact amount to put in a cocktail. Another example relates to the recipe for our Cable Car cocktail, which traditionally uses curaçao. We found the standard curaçao options to be too sweet for the cocktail and, after stumbling upon and testing Pierre Ferrand® Dry curaçao, find it to be perfect for that cocktail.

- You can make most cocktails with a relatively short list of support ingredients that are easy to find. Certain ingredients like Angostura® bitters, club soda, oranges, lemons, limes, and bottled cocktail cherries are used in many cocktails and should be kept handy. Fortunately, they keep well over time—especially if the fruits are refrigerated.

- Some ingredients that are a bit putzy, or that must gestate for a long time, are a little more complicated, but worth it. Examples include the Damn Near Perfect® Top Shelf Margarita that steeps overnight, and the Falernum that is key to the Damn Near Perfect® Mai Tai and is used in a variety of other cocktails as well.

- Balance is the key to all DNP™ cocktails. If they are too sweet or too tart, they just don't work. We believe when people say they don't like "sweet cocktails," they usually mean they do not like cocktails that are overly sweet. Sweetness can be modified not only by the volume of sweetener used but also by the strength of the sweetener. Some of our recipes call for 1:1 simple syrup, and others call for the less sweet 2:1 simple syrup. If you are testing, and believe your tested version is "too sweet," try toning down the sweetness rather than just discarding the cocktail altogether.

- More is not always better! For example, do NOT put large slices of lemon peel in a Martini. There's a reason the recipe calls for a "twist."

- We hope you will enjoy your own testings and find they lead to great experiences with your friends and excellent cocktails you all can enjoy for a long time!

APPENDIX FOUR

Equipment needed to make Damn Near Perfect® Cocktails

Almost all Damn Near Perfect® cocktails can be made using equipment, utensils, and miscellaneous items commonly found in your home kitchen (such things as blenders, toothpicks, strainers, a variety of glassware, etc.). Other items that some kitchens may not contain can facilitate the ease of making a couple of the DNP™ cocktails. These include a mandoline, which makes it very easy to slice things thinly (but can be substituted by a sharp knife), and an electric juicing machine (its function can be met in other ways). It is not essential to spend a lot of money to have on hand what is needed to make the cocktails in this book. The photo highlights some tools worth having in your cocktail arsenal:

1. A **Microplane®** is very nice to have as it facilitates grating nutmeg and zesting lemon and lime peels. Microplanes® are inexpensive and come in a variety of styles. We find the one in the photo to be useful for cocktails and some food items.

2. The **hand citrus squeezer** shown makes juicing lemons and limes very easy—and can be found for less than $10.

3. **Cocktail shakers** come in a wide variety of sizes and shapes. We use the one shown extensively as it easily makes 1 to 2 cocktails. It, too, can be found in some places for under $10. We have two, the larger version works well for cocktail parties.

4. From our viewpoint, shot glasses, with the ounce measurements shown, are essential. They, too, are very inexpensive.

5. **Muddlers** are very useful for making several DNP™ cocktails and, although cocktails can be muddled using the back of a spoon, and in other ways, we recommend investing in a good muddler, which will not cost much.

6. A **hand immersion mixer** makes it much easier to get egg whites to a nice froth. If you wish to bypass this tool, you can get decent froth by shaking the egg whites for a long time prior to putting ice into the shaker.

7. A **blender** is the only way we would make our DNP™ Ramos Gin Fizz but, as most homes have one, this should not present a problem.

8. A nice **cocktail spoon**, though not critical to own, is so inexpensive it is worth the investment.

9. An **electric juicer** is particularly useful for juicing apples and pineapples, though there are workarounds if one does not wish to invest in one.

APPENDIX FIVE

Ingredients for Damn Near Perfect Cocktails ®
(Alphabetically)

SPIRITS

American Whiskey
- Jack Daniel's®
- Michter's® Single Barrel Straight Rye

Bourbon
- Blanton's®
- Buffalo Trace®
- Evan Williams®
- Michter's® Kentucky Straight Bourbon
- Noah's Mill®

Calvados
- Boulard® Grand Solage Pays d'Auge
- Calvados du Pays d'Auge Reserve

Canadian Whiskey
- Canadian Club®
- Crown Royal®

Champagne
- Piper Heidsieck® NV

Cognac
- Courvoisier® VSOP
- Hennessey® VS
- Remy Martin® VSOP

Gin
- Beefeater®
- Bombay®
- Bombay Sapphire®
- Gordon's®
- Tanqueray®

Irish Whiskey
- Jameson Irish Whiskey®

Pisco
- Capel®
- Horcon Quemado® 40

Rum
- Bacardi® Gold Rum
- Bacardi® Superior White Rum
- Captain Morgan®
- Havana Club® (white)
- Myers's® Original Dark Rum
- Sailor Jerry's®

Tequila/Mescal

- 100 Años Sauza® Tequila
- 1800® Reposado Tequila
- Conmemorativo® Tequila
- Kirkland® 100% Agave Tequila Blanco
- Monte Alban Mescal®
- Sacrificio Mescal®

Vermouth

- Noilly Prat® Rouge (i.e., sweet)
- Noilly Prat® Original Dry
- Punt e Mes®

Vodka

- Bak's® Zubrowka Bison Grass
- Ketel One Citroen®
- Smirnoff® Number 21 Triple Distilled Red Label

LIQUEURS

- Absente®
- Ancho Reyes Verde® Poblano
- Aperol®
- Bailey's®
- Berentzen®
- Bols®
- Campari®
- Chartreuse®
- Cocci® Americano
- Cointreau®
- De Kuyper® dark crème de cacao
- Grand Marnier®

- Kahlua®
- Luxardo®
- Midori®
- Partus 68 Absinthe
- Pernod®
- Pierre Ferrand® Dry Curacao
- Schöanauer Apfel
- Torres® "Gran Torres" orange liqueur

NON-ALCOHOL INGREDIENTS

Bitters
- Angostura® bitters
- Peychaud® bitters

Frozen Concentrates
- Minute Maid® frozen lemonade concentrate
- Minute Maid® frozen limeade concentrate

Ice Cream
- Graeter's® vanilla
- Haagen-Dazs® vanilla

Liquids
- Ocean Spray® Cranberry Juice Cocktail
- R.W. Knudsen® "Just Tart Cherry" juice
- Schweppes® club soda
- Rose flower water
- Orange blossom water

Miscellaneous
- Bada Bing Cherries®
- El Yucateco® Chili Habanero Sauce

Syrups

- Agave syrup
- D'Arbo® elderflower syrup
- Ginger syrup

Tonic

- Schweppes®

Also, a variety of fresh fruits, spices, vegetables, etc., as shown in the recipes.

APPENDIX SIX

Holders of Trademarks

10 Cane® .... Moet Hennessy PTE LTD

100 Años Sauza®............................... Tequila Sauza, S. de R.L. de C.V.

1800® .... Tequila Cuervo Rojena, S.A. de C.V.

Absente® .... Absente®, LLC

Alto del Carmen .... Cooperativa Agricola Pisquera Elqui Limitada

Ancho Reyes Verde .... Licorera Ancho Reyes y Cia, S.A. P.I. de C.V.

Angostura®... Angostura International

Aperol... Davide Campari–Milano N.V.

Bacardi®... Bacardi & Company Limited

Bada Bing Cherries®.......................... Metzger Specialty Brands, Inc.

Bak's Bison Grass Vodka® .... A&A Lazur Corporation

Beefeater®.......................... Allied Domecq Spirits and Wine Limited

Berentzen® .... Berentzen-Gruppe AG

Bittermens .... Bittermens LLC

Blanton's® .... Age International, Inc.

Bombay® .... Bacardi & Company Limited

Bombay Sapphire® .... Bacardi & Company Limited

Boulard® Calvados.. SACB

Buffalo Trace .... Sazerac Brands LLC

Campari... Davide Campari–Milano N.V.

Canada Dry®... Dr. Pepper/Seven Up, Inc.

Canadian Club®.................................... Canadian Club Canada Inc.

Capel®........................... Cooperative Agricola Pisquera Elqui Ltda

Captain Morgan® .... Diageo North America, Inc.

Chartreuse .... Chartreuse Corporation

Citroen . . . . Double Eagle Brands

Cocchi® (Americano). . . . . Giulio Cocchi Spumanti S.R.L.

Cointreau® . . . . Cointreau Société par actions simplifiée

Confidencial . . . . Casa Santos Lima–Companhia das inhas

Courvoisier® VSOP. . . . . Couvoisier S.A.S. Societe

Crown Royal®. . . . . Diageo North America, Inc.

Crystal® *Symphony*. . . . . .Crystal Cruises, Inc.

Damn Near Perfect® . . . . Berdie, Douglas R.

D'Arbo®. . . . . Adolf D'Arbo AG Corporation

De Kuyper . . . . .Koninklijke De Kuyper B.V. TA De Kuyper Royal Distillers

Dewer's . . . . Bacardi & Company Limited

Dolin . . . . .Dolin

Earl Giles . . . . Earl Giles Bottling Company

El Yucateco® . . . . .Priamo J. Gamboa S.A. DE C.V.

Evan Williams . . . . Heaven Hill Distilleries

Fentimans® . . . . Fentimans Limited

Fever-Tree® . . . . Fevertree Limited

Foco. . . . . Thai Agri Foods Public Company Limited

Glenfiddich . . . . William Grant & Sons Limited

Gordon's. . . . . Diageo Brands B.V.

Goya. . . . . Goya Foods, Inc.

Graeter's® . . . . .Graeter's Inc.

Grand Marnier®. . . . . Societe des Produits Marnier-Lapostolle

Haagan-Dazs® . . . . .HDIP, Inc.

Havana Club®. . . . . Havana Club Holdings S.A.

Hennessy® V.S. . . . . .Moet Hennessy USA, Inc.

Isle of Bute . . . . Isle of Bute Gin Co.

Jack Daniels® . . . . .Jack Daniel's Properties, Inc.

Jameson Irish Whiskey® . . . . .Irish Distillers Limited

Jarritos Toronja. . . . . Jarritos, Inc.

Jumex .... Commercialization Eloro, S.A.

Jungle Pulp .... C.A. Spice, Inc.

Jura .... Jura Elecktroapparate A G

Kahlua. .... The Absolut Company Aktiebolag

Ketel One Citroen® Vodka .... Double Eagle Brands B.V.

Kirkland®. .... Costco Wholesale Corporation

Lillet®. .... Societe Lillet Freres

Luxardo .... Girolamo Luxardo S.P.A.

Magdala .... Miguel Torres, S.A.

Martinelli's Gold Medal Cider .... S. Martinelli & Company

Metusalem .... Ron Metusalem & Matusa of Florida, Inc.

Michter's .... JNJ Enterprises, LLC

Microplane® .... Grace Manufacturing Inc.

Midori. .... Suntory Holdings Limited

Minute Maid®. .... The Coca-Cola Company

Monte Alban®. .... Sazerac North America, Inc.

Myers's® Original Dark Rum .... Diageo North America, Inc.

Noah's Mill® .... Kentucky Bourbon Distillers, Ltd.

Noilly Prat®. .... Etalissements Noilly Prat & CIE

Ocean Spray® Cranberry Juice Cocktail .... Ocean Spray Cranberries, Inc.

Pernod® .... Ricard S.A.

Peychaud® bitters .... Sazerac Co., Inc.

Pierre Ferrand® Dry Curacao. .... Cognac Ferrand

Piper Heidsieck®. .... Compagnie Champenoise PH-CH. Piper Heidsieck

Plum Fu-Kui .... Matsui Shuzo

Punt e Mes. .... Punt.Mes

Q® .... Q Tonic LLC

Remy Martin® VSOP .... E. Remy Martin & Co.

R.W. Knudsen® "Just Tart Cherry .... Smucker Natural Foods, Inc. Sailor

Sauza. .... Tequila Sauza, S. de R.L. de C.V.

APPENDIX SEVEN

Prayer of Self-Forgiveness for Not Being Perfect

Lord,

Please help me to forgive myself for not being perfect,

And help me remember that the love of my friends
 and family

Has nothing to do with perfection.

Furthermore, remind me that those friends
 and family members neither

Expect, nor want, me to be perfect because of
the burden it would impose on them.

Also, please remind me that my parents did not
expect perfection of me,

Merely asking that I be a good person and
help others.

Help me to remember that by making mistakes
I learn, and that

If I were perfect, my learning would cease,
and I would become a boring drudge.

Help me to laugh at the mistakes I do make
and smile at them,

Knowing that I am learning in the process.

Thank you, Lord.

D. Berdie (2013)

ACKNOWLEDGMENTS

Primary acknowledgment goes to two family members. My wife Elaine agreed to put up with about ten years of zaniness associated with this project and then, willingly, agreed to participate in the extensive testing that was required over those years. Our son Ray provided extensive professional guidance and support on business and technological issues.

Phil Eckhert provided phenomenal photographic support (both in terms of the incredible photography and his patience throughout the project). Elise Walker designed and finalized the first edition, which made it possible for us to move forward. And Gary Lindberg did a great job of juggling the format of the first edition of the book with this new expanded edition so they fit well together. To them goes my heartiest thanks!

And most recently, my editor Pat Morris provided the incredible professional support without which this second edition of *Damn Near Perfect Cocktails*™ would not have been possible. We should all toast her every time we raise a glass!

Finally, our thanks to the many cocktail pioneers who have preceded us and who laid the groundwork upon which we have built. Consultation from professional bartenders we have known is also fully appreciated. Bradley, who helped us refine several cocktails while we were cruising on the Crystal® *Symphony*, is always fondly in our hearts.

ABOUT THE AUTHOR

Doug is not a professional bartender. He is like many of you who enjoy cocktails and wish to have a core set of them you can make with reliable, satisfying results. Doug has a PhD in Philosophy and heavy experience in sociology and marketing research. He's written dozens of professional articles on how to conduct reliable and valid research. Hence, along with his wife Elaine, who has a PhD in Psychology, the testing and refinement of the cocktail recipes in this book meet scientific standards for reliability. It was hard work, but they figured "someone had to do it!"

Elaine and Doug Berdie, left, with Phil Eckhert.

www.ingramcontent.com/pod-product-compliance
Lightning Source LLC
Chambersburg PA
CBHW042239140626
46547CB00036B/27